BODIES
in Motion

Finding Joy in Fitness

by GILAD JANKLOWICZ
and ANN MARIE BROWN

Foghorn
Press Inc.

ISBN 0-935701-55-9

51495 >

9 780935 701555

Foghorn Press, Inc.
555 DeHaro Street
The Boiler Room #220
San Francisco, CA 94107
(415) 241-9550

Library of Congress
Cataloging-in-Publication Data:

Janklowicz, Gilad

Bodies in Motion / by Gilad Janklowicz and Ann Marie Brown
p. cm.

ISBN 0-935701-55-9 : $14.95

1. Physical fitness.   2. Nutrition.   3. Health
I. Ann Marie Brown   II. Title

GV481.J36   1993
613.7—dc20

92-2440 CIP

Printed in the United States of America.

BODIES
in Motion

Finding Joy in Fitness

---

by GILAD JANKLOWICZ
and ANN MARIE BROWN

Foghorn
Press
Inc.

Book Credits

Book Design: Curium Design and I. Magnus
Editorial: Thomas Holton, Howard Rabinowitz, Nina Schuyler, Ethan Watters

Photo Credits

Front Cover: Ric Noyle
Back Cover: Hank Londoner
Color Section: (in order of pages)
        1) Hank Londoner
        2) top—Hank Londoner / lower—Asher Okada
        3) all—Hank Londoner
        4) Hank Londoner
        5) all—Ric Noyle
        6) top and lower left—Ric Noyle / lower right—Hank Londoner
        7) top—Ric Noyle / lower—Hank Londoner
        8) top left and right—Hank Londoner / lower—Ric Noyle

All black and white photos in this book are the work of Ric Noyle except as noted:
        Page 7—Steven DeParis
        Page 157—Hank Londoner
        About the Authors page—Hank Londoner (left photo) and Lex Fletcher (right photo)

Acknowledgements

I would like to acknowledge and thank the following people, whose contributions were integral to this book:

Rick Carroll, Marie DeParis, George Fuller, Russ Hodge, Thomas Holton, Erwin Jaskulski, Jim Karanas, Hank Londoner, Ric Noyle, and Joe Theismann.

This book is dedicated to my friends, family and fellow workers who have supported, inspired and believed in me through my pursuit of the "Bodies in Motion" program. Without them, I could not have made this dream into a reality.

And to the many participating "Bodies in Motion" viewers and students, whose success stories keep me motivated.

CONTENTS

Joe Theismann is a two-time Pro Bowl player and the most productive quarterback in the history of the Washington Redskins. After a 12-year NFL career, Joe Theismann joined ESPN as an expert analyst for Sunday night nationally televised NFL games. He is also a businessman and motivational lecturer.

While I was growing up in South River, New Jersey, people would always tell me that I would never succeed as an athlete because I was so small. Yes, I was a skinny little kid, but what I didn't have in size, I made up for in motivation. Nothing motivates me more than someone telling me, "You can't do that." If I was challenged to do ten push-ups, I'd do eleven.

As we get older, our challenges are greater, but it's that same motivation that I felt as a kid that has helped me overcome the adversity that I, and all of us, face in our everyday lives.

On November 18, 1985, I suffered an injury that proved to be the end of my professional football career. But at the time, I couldn't accept that my playing days were over. I spent every waking moment rehabilitating, exercising and working harder than I had ever worked in my life to overcome the physical challenge that faced me. Although I was not able to play football again, I know that the physical abilities I have now are due to the fact that I didn't give up—that I continued to challenge myself despite the limits that were put on me.

I can't stress enough the importance of physical fitness. Our bodies are the machines we rely on to get us through each day. All the successful people I know, whether they are in the world of sports or in the world of business, realize the importance of keeping fit. A healthy body supplies us with the energy we need to meet life's challenges. When our bodies are in the best possible condition, we feel better about ourselves, and when we feel good about ourselves, we can accomplish things we never thought possible. Good health is a precious commodity that should never be taken for granted.

I know it's been said before, but the hardest part is taking that first step. I guarantee that once you take that first exercise class, or get in that first workout, or take that first jog, the high that you achieve will keep you coming back for more. Just be sure not to expect too much too soon. How often have we walked into a gym, seen all the strong, fit bodies, and felt like giving up in discouragement? Instead, we need to look at those same people for inspiration and know that with the same amount of dedication and perseverance, we too can achieve our goals.

By reading this book, you have taken the first step toward becoming the best that you can be. There is no one more qualified to teach us, inspire us and motivate us than Gilad Janklowicz. His enthusiasm and expertise are surpassed only by his genuine desire to educate people on the importance of physical fitness.

When Gil asked me to be on his *Bodies in Motion* show, many people were skeptical. Football players aren't exactly known for their graceful style. Most of my friends were afraid I'd embarrass myself. But I was excited about taking on a new challenge, and I've had a great time on the show. As I learned in the world of sports, life is very competitive. We have to learn to have confidence in ourselves and believe that we can accomplish whatever we set our minds to. If we wait for someone else to give us that confidence, chances are it will never happen.

As you start out on your new challenge, remember that there are no shortcuts. There is no substitute for hard work and persistence. But the reward is invaluable—you're going to achieve a healthy body and mind, and the knowledge that you can accomplish whatever you want to.

—Joe Theismann, November 1992

Every book has a beginning, and this book began with my friend Erwin Jaskulski. Erwin lives here in Honolulu, and I met him one day while I was running on the beach near Waikiki.

I'm always interested in talking to people who are involved in fitness, so I was intrigued by the sight of this older man training vigorously at the beach park. I watched him run, do some chin-ups on a bar, drop to the ground for some push-ups, and then take a long swim in the ocean. All of this he did with great intensity and enthusiasm. Finally, I went over to him and asked him how old he was.

He laughed at my curiosity. "Everyone asks me that! I'm 83 years old."

Well, that was several years ago, and since then Erwin and I have become good friends. These days we sometimes work out on the beach together, and Erwin is now in his nineties.

I must admit that I wanted to know Erwin's secret—how did he manage to stay so fit, healthy and motivated at his age? But Erwin will tell you he knows no secrets—he simply has learned to find the joy in everything he does.

Not just physically active, Erwin also reads three hours a day, speaks five languages, subscribes to twelve magazines, and collects music and books. That's in addition to his daily workouts which include running, swimming, calisthenics, climbing stairs, and hiking in the mountains. "This, plus a few household chores, fills a whole day," Erwin says with a smile.

"You improve the world best by improving yourself," he tells me. And he never stops trying to improve. The last time I saw him, he was excited because he had just done 11 chin-ups instead of his usual ten. He goes to the beach daily for a three-mile walk/run, 15 minutes of calisthenics, and a quarter-mile swim. "At my age," he laughs, "just keeping up is improving."

And so over the years, Erwin has become my mentor. Every time I see him, I am reminded to live life with enthusiasm. Erwin helps me remember to find the joy in all my activities, including my workouts. And as Erwin says, the best way to enjoy life is to maintain a finely tuned mind and body.

This book is about pursuing your personal best and having fun doing it. I believe that with good nutrition and an exercise program, you can not only add years to your life, you can add life to your years. Just like Erwin.

So let's go do it—

Gilad

Motivation

At left, Erwin Jaskulski and Gilad do a few chin-ups during their morning training on the beach.

Above, Erwin and Gilad running at the beach park.

A body at rest tends to stay at rest and a body in motion tends to stay in motion unless acted upon by external forces. That is Newton's law of inertia and momentum. A rock stays motionless unless something or someone forces it from its resting position. When it comes to human beings, the force that can move us comes from our minds—that force is our motivation.

When I came up with the name "Bodies in Motion" for my exercise program, I was thinking about how we are all a part of the universe and that the universe is in motion. Look around you—planets, stars and galaxies are all in motion and living things are in motion, too.

Human beings are meant to be in motion. Our early ancestors were extremely active every day—they had to be, in order to find food and shelter. They couldn't just go shopping in the supermarket and drive home to prepare a meal. Their "supermarket" was their environment and their legs were their means of transportation. Sometimes they ran to catch their food and other times they ran so they wouldn't become food. Their bodies were conditioned to operate at peak performance, out of the simple need for survival.

But technology and progress have brought us a long way from the days of hunting and gathering. Now, most of us practice "survival" techniques by sitting at our desks and struggling to bring home our paychecks, or racing through the intersection trying to beat the red light. Being fit, which in earlier days of human evolution was a function of survival and necessity, has become in modern times a function of leisure time and awareness.

I believe we all have an innate ability to live our lives as fit and healthy people. Our bodies possess inherent wisdom about how we best can thrive in the world, culled from thousands of years of human evolution. This information is passed on from generation to generation through our genetic coding. I believe that all we have to do is tap into that inner knowledge, and then our natural abilities will propel us toward living fit and healthy lives.

We all possess this universal wisdom. It's our birthright, given to us to use in a positive manner. What we do with this gift in our conscious lives, and how well we take care of it as we journey through life, is up to every one of us individually.

We're All Natural Athletes

I believe we are all "natural athletes," and our bodies are just waiting for the opportunity to exercise their innate physical abilities. However, somewhere along the way many of us have forgotten these abilities. We forgot them because we didn't use them. Maybe as youngsters we experienced "failure" at sports, or we never received the right instruction and got frustrated. Or maybe we just never had any good physically fit role models in our families—so exercise and athletics became pursuits for "other people." Many people have pushed sports and fitness aside, assuming they are not for them because they have never competed or played on a team and enjoyed it.

In recent years in Hawaii, I have noticed a growing number of people are participating in various team sports and even grueling triathlons. Many of these people are in sports for the first time in their lives. At a mature age,

> *A body at rest tends to stay at rest, and a body in motion tends to stay in motion.*

they have decided to give sports and fitness a shot. It's beautiful to see these people setting goals and achieving their personal best.

Everyone wants to improve their abilities and become better, to expand their potential and achieve their goals. It's what progress is all about, and this drive to improve is what pushes us forward, both as individuals and as a society. We are happy with ourselves when we achieve something, whether it is on a grand scale or on a small one. Whether we build a castle on a hill or grow a rose in our backyard, whether we win an Olympic gold medal or make the cut on our local bowling team, it's all about achievement, and achievement is about putting energy into motion.

Awareness

Before you can get in motion you need drive, and before you have drive, you need desire. Desire stems from mental awareness, the awareness of knowing what is good for you in your life. It's an outlook—an understanding of what is positive and worth having. Becoming aware of the things you want to achieve can make the difference between reaching your potential and letting it waste away. Awareness creates desire, desire creates drive, and drive sets us in motion. Motion will direct you to expend your energy, and by expending your energy on a regular basis, and with direction, you will be moving forward toward achieving your goals.

Mental awareness means making a positive lifestyle choice, setting realistic goals and achieving your personal best. Reaching the desired mental awareness is actually more important than achieving a perfect body. Trying to be perfect is not your goal. Of course no one is perfect, but trying to bring out the best attributes of yourself is a goal worth pursuing.

I see people lavishing so much care and attention on material things. They take perfect care of their cars and buy only the best clothes, but when it comes to taking care of themselves, the picture could be a lot brighter. It never ceases to amaze me how much attention, time and effort we are willing to spend on "things," yet when it comes to our health, we put ourselves last. We take our health for granted or we don't pay it the attention it deserves.

Taking care of ourselves will actually allow us to take better care of the things we care about. When we develop an awareness of what is good for us, we can create for ourselves optimal conditions for our lives. Only from a firm foundation can we reach for our personal best.

Making the Commitment

Only you can start the ball rolling on the way to a fitter and healthier lifestyle, and only you can decide that the commitment and dedication are worth the benefits and results. The best motivation for fitness is knowing the benefits and joy it will bring you.

Here are some of the benefits of a fit lifestyle:

- ▶ *greater confidence and self-esteem*
- ▶ *renewed energy*
- ▶ *improvement in overall appearance*
- ▶ *increased strength and endurance*
- ▶ *better overall health*
- ▶ *better blood circulation*
- ▶ *increased metabolic rate*
- ▶ *more efficient and stronger heart*
- ▶ *lowered blood pressure*

Achievement is about putting energy into motion.

▶ *healthier mix of cholesterol levels*
▶ *increased muscle mass and less fat*
▶ *lowered blood sugar level*
▶ *increased endorphin level*
▶ *reduced risk of disease and illness*

Momentum

We all know what it's like to play on a playground swing. When you start swinging, building height on your swing takes some effort. But then as you start swinging higher, the effort becomes easier. You can swing very high with very little effort as long as you keep your momentum going. Once your momentum stops, you and the swing will come back to a resting position. And then if you start swinging again, you'll have to start all over again from the beginning. Just because you swung before doesn't mean that on your next swinging session you'll start from the highest point. You'll have to use effort and momentum to return to that point.

The same applies to your fitness program. If you are starting a program or increasing the intensity of your program, there will always be an initial period of accomodation and discomfort, until the body and the mind adjust to new demands. It doesn't matter if you are a beginner or an advanced exerciser—if you start a program, change your program or increase the intensity of your existing program, you'll have to go through a period of adjustment to new demands.

This period should not last more than about three to four weeks. But

> *Exercising regularly gives you a wonderful sense of self-control.*

as you "stick it out" and work towards your goal, you are building momentum. Soon you realize that you are working at the level you set out to achieve—it has become more familiar and it takes a little less effort to do the same tasks that several weeks earlier you could only imagine doing.

I'll make a bet with you: If you begin and stick to an exercise program, if you follow it regularly for three to six months, you will find that you've built momentum into your life. In fact, I'll up the wager and bet that once you've built some momentum, you'll feel better and look better than you ever have.

Gaining Control

Finding out you have the perseverance to stick with an exercise program is a powerful discovery—it means you possess a tool that can get you through some of the toughest times of life. You see, the strength you develop by sticking to your exercise routine—even if you don't feel like doing it that day, or even if there are other things you could do instead—is the same strength that gives you control over other areas of your life. Exercising regularly gives you a wonderful sense of self-control, as well as boosting your self-confidence and self-esteem. Let's be honest: it takes a fair amount of self-discipline to exercise regularly, especially in the beginning when it feels uncomfortable and your muscles get sore easily and you think that everyone else is much more advanced than you are. But people who have done it—people who have gotten past this first stage—all have similar stories to tell. People who set and achieve physical goals discover time and time again that by tapping into their powers of perseverance and strength to do so, they suddenly realize greater success in other areas of their lives, whether it's building a stronger marriage or advancing in a career.

The only way for you to gain control in your life is to start by mastering your own body. The pursuit of health and fitness is a great way to get you on the track, because when it comes to fitness, you get back what you put into it and more.

Mapping Your Program

There are three important factors to consider when mapping out your program. They are crucial to keeping you inspired and motivated:

1—Set realistic goals. Start with a goal you can achieve—work within your own ability to perform. Accomplishing a worthwhile goal takes time. When it comes to your health and fitness, there are no shortcuts and no miracles. Instead, you need to take a step-by-step approach, setting small goals and achieving them one by one. A series of small accomplishments over time will bring on big improvements before you even realize it.

2—Take a positive approach. Accept yourself. If you are not where you want to be in your fitness level, or with your dietary habits, it's only because it wasn't important enough for you until now. Don't judge yourself. If you accept yourself fully, you will be able to make positive changes in your life more easily. Maybe you haven't been exercising. Maybe you haven't been eating well. Let it go—it's done. It was your choice. But now you can make other choices, and better ones, too.

Try to approach your actions with a smile and optimism. Research shows that optimism increases our chances of living longer and healthier lives. Doctors and scientists are paying more respect to the power and potential of optimistic thinking. We can't change yesterday, but we can definitely make positive decisions that will improve tomorrow.

3—Measure the goals you set. The best way to stay on track and be able to see your progress is to set goals you can accomplish and measure. That way, you can actually see your progress taking place. When I decided it was time to cut down on my coffee intake, I looked at where I was and where I wanted to be. My starting position was six to nine cups of coffee a day. My first goal, over a period of two weeks, was to drink coffee only with meals and to have only one or one and a half cups per meal.

After two weeks, I noticed that I could handle that, so I proceeded to my next measurable goal: I had one cup of coffee for every two meals. After another two weeks of being able to accomplish this, I set my final measurable goal. Now I'll have only one cup of coffee a day, and only in the morning.

By taking controlled and measurable steps to achieving your goals, you can alter, change or eliminate bad habits. Through the same process, you can also introduce and cultivate new good habits in your life.

Until you realize that denial and drastic change is not the way to go, you will constantly find yourself on a merry-go-round of attempted self-improvement followed by backsliding, feeling guilty and then finally giving up. In the case of dieting, when you deny yourself all the foods you like, lose weight, then crave those foods and gain all the weight back, the merry-go-round gets

> *Start with a goal you can achieve— work within your own ability to perform.*

harder and harder to control and riskier for your health.

Instead you need to slowly start gaining control of your weight and fitness level by switching gradually from foods that you know are bad for you to foods that you know are good for you. Just as you can train and improve your body, you can also train your taste buds and improve your diet. You can make big improvements by applying and measuring small changes in both your fitness program and your nutrition plan.

Define Your Goals

Getting fit requires that you get your body in motion. In order to determine your specific motion, you need to define your goals. What is it you want from a fitness program? What do you want to achieve or improve? What kind of lifestyle changes do you need to make to accommodate your goals? Is it possible for you to make those changes on an on-going basis?

Hitting a target you can't see is always a difficult proposition. You need to be very clear on what you are going after. Instead of saying, "I want to get in better shape," you should set a more clearly defined goal—one that you can measure. Choose one (or a few) very precise small goals. Do you want to start a walking/running program three times a week? Do you want to run a 10K race in 45 minutes? Do you want to lose some body fat? Do you want

> *You can make big improve-ments by applying and measuring small changes.*

to lower your blood pressure? Do you want to eat a higher fiber diet? Do you want to drink less alcohol?

Decide on a few changes you want to make. What specifically do you want to get out of your own health and fitness program?

Build Success into the Process

Be careful not to start with a goal that seems very difficult or unattainable. The key to making any change in your life is to build success into the process, so choose a goal that is within your reach—one that you can succeed at. Start with small goals, achieve small successes; move on to larger goals, achieve larger successes. With a continual series of successes behind you, you will feel positive and motivated toward further success. Winners seldom get discouraged.

I tried this technique myself, although I didn't know I was doing it at the time. I was training for the decathlon and there was one event I really struggled with: the 110-meter high hurdles. I tried and tried, but I just couldn't clear those hurdles as easily as I needed to. Then one day my coach had me train with the hurdles set at a much lower height. I was able to clear the lower height easily, which helped build up my confidence.

Slowly I started to increase the height of the hurdles. I wouldn't raise them until I could easily clear them with confidence, several times in a row. Soon enough, I could clear the hurdles set at their regular height, and it was because I had allowed myself to achieve success.

By building success instead of frustration into my training, I gained the confidence necessary to keep going and achieve my goal. The moral of the story is don't try to achieve too much too soon and don't try to outdo yourself. When you train within your limits, you train smart. You build confidence through repetition and consistency and your overall performance improves.

Goals and Lifestyle Changes

So, first you need to identify the health and fitness goals you want to achieve. Then, identify the lifestyle changes you can make to achieve those goals. Be sure that your lifestyle changes are not ones that seem impossible to you. Remember, you want to build success into your program. Here are some examples of clearly defined goals and the lifestyle changes that could help you achieve them:

▶**Goal:** I want to cut down on the amount of red meat I eat.
▶**Lifestyle Change:** I will eat red meat only once a week, and the rest of the time I will substitute chicken or fish.

▶**Goal:** I want to exercise more than I do now, which is only about twice a week.
▶**Lifestyle Change:** I will set aside three weekday mornings where I will get up 45 minutes earlier to walk/jog. I will also exercise one hour on the weekend.

▶**Goal:** I want to cut down on my snacking so I can lose a little extra weight.
▶**Lifestyle Change:** I especially like to have snacks at night, so I will save my snacking for the evening and I will switch from potato chips and corn chips to a bowl of fresh fruit and a couple of whole wheat crackers.

Take Action

Now comes the action. If you have more than one goal you want to achieve, I recommend that you implement only one lifestyle change at a time, especially if the changes seem like they will be difficult for you to make. Making one change at a time and succeeding at it will be far more motivating than trying to do everything at once and becoming overwhelmed or discouraged.

When implementing changes in your schedule to accommodate a new fitness program, plan the changes so you can easily incorporate them. Don't fall into the trap of scheduling a workout at a time that you know won't work for you. Or if you've been addicted to sweets all your life, don't think that going "cold turkey" is the only way to stop the habit. Allow for the fact that as human beings, we respond best to gradual changes in our lifestyles.

Monitor Your Progress

Monitor your progress week by week. How are you doing? Remember that you do not develop new habits overnight. If a few weeks have passed and you've been unsuccessful at implementing your lifestyle change, maybe you need to re-examine that change. It may be that the goal you chose was worthwhile, but the lifestyle change you chose to implement is simply not workable for you. Remember, there is no such thing as failure in your fitness plan. You just have to find the right approach.

For example, perhaps you realize that your goal to start exercising more by getting up early two mornings a week is too difficult, because you can't stand getting up earlier. Let's face it—you're just not a morning person. So instead, you could decide to start exercis-

Allow for the fact that as human beings, we respond best to gradual changes in our lifestyles.

ing for an hour at lunch three days a week. A few weeks later you may see that this lifestyle change really works; you love getting out of the office for your lunchtime workouts.

The bottom line is that we can all achieve pretty good results for ourselves in health and fitness if we only make the simple choice that yes, it is important and yes, I can find a way to incorporate fitness into my lifestyle.

Encourage Yourself

Don't forget to encourage yourself. It is easy to overlook our small successes, and not give ourselves the credit we deserve. Congratulate yourself for all those small changes and successful steps. And if you don't achieve your goal right away, don't give in to discouragement, because change, large or small, is never an easy process. There are always pitfalls along the way. If you can't follow your fitness program one day for whatever reason, don't feel guilty about it. Let it go and start fresh the next day. Allow yourself the benefit of being able to start again. Do not wallow in self-criticism or harsh self-judgement, and don't let anything make you give up your goal.

I've seen too many people start a program and then give it up because they slacked off for a couple of days and now feel that they can't trust themselves. Let go of self-judgement, and allow the next moment to be a fresh start.

Don't forget to encourage yourself.

No Competition

For as many billions of people there are in the world, there is only one like you. Doesn't that thought turn you on? Becoming the best YOU in the world is a tremendous goal and only you can achieve it. If you fall into the trap of comparing yourself to others, you will always be somewhat frustrated because no matter how good you are, there will always be someone out there who is stronger than you, faster than you, or somehow better than you are.

Forget about all the other competition out there. Your job is to achieve your personal best, which has nothing to do with what anyone else can achieve.

Compare the difference between a competitive athlete—whose bottom line is winning—and a person who is incorporating fitness into his life for the sole reason of bettering himself and looking for the joy in health and fitness. There is a vast difference between these two approaches. The difference lies in doing it without the pressure of having to do it. A competitive athlete puts in a lot of hours and hard work specifically focused toward the goal of achieving success in competition. The athlete must push himself beyond his limit on a regular basis. When you are participating in activities for the sake of staying in shape and maintaining a healthy lifestyle, you don't need to push that hard. Your goals are enjoyment and better health and self-improvement.

A competitive athlete's energy is focused on winning in competition with others. When pursuing a program for health and fitness, you are improving yourself so you can win in competition with yourself and become better than you were yesterday. Of course, you have goals you want to achieve, and for some people, getting into a competition with others can help them stay motivated about their goals. Some people really enjoy the added pressure of preparing for a weekend 10K race or an evening team sports league. But overall, reaching for your personal best without comparing yourself to others and finding the joy in your workout program is what your goal should be.

How to Stay Motivated

Here are some suggestions to help you stay motivated on your fitness program:

▶**Exercise in the way that is most fun for you.** Exercise is important, necessary and something people should do on a regular basis, but it should also be fun—something you enjoy doing. If it's not fun, you won't be able to make it part of your lifestyle. How do you make it fun? For starters, you should choose a form of exercise you like to do. If you really don't like the way running feels, try swimming or cycling or weight lifting or anything else.

From there, you want to make your form of exercise as pleasant as possible. You may find that you prefer exercising with a friend, so you can encourage and support each other. You're far less likely to cancel an exercise session if someone else is relying on you to be there. People who exercise in groups are generally better able to sustain their exercise programs over time.

You may find that you like exercising to music, as music can be very relaxing and can divert your attention from the hard work you are doing.

And don't forget that to keep it fun, you have to stay in control of your program and not let your program control you. Always work within your own limitations—don't try to do too much too soon. Start with a level you know you can meet—don't set your standard higher than your abilities at the moment.

More than once I've seen guys who remember what they bench-pressed in high school during their football days, and now, fifteen to twenty years later, they bet each other to prove they can still do it. Of course, that can be an unrealistic and ultimately frustrating goal. Don't let your mind set contracts your body can't meet. Start your program by doing something you can finish, not something that will finish you.

▶**Get trained or train yourself.** Consider hiring a personal trainer to work with you, teach you and motivate you. Or you may want to be your own personal trainer—monitoring yourself through your workout, keeping records of when you worked out, what exercises you performed, how much weight you lifted, how far you ran and what your time was. See page 44 for a sample training log that you can copy and use.

It's great to keep records on paper. In your mind, it's easy to lose track of how far you've come, but when it is written down, you can really see how much you've improved.

▶**Schedule it in.** Definitely schedule a time for your exercise activities. It should be written right there, in your appointment book, just the same as taking your kids to piano lessons or meeting with the chairman of the board. You will always be able to think of a good reason to skip a workout or to not eat a healthful meal. There are always things to be done that

> *Don't let your mind set contracts your body can't meet.*

seem more pressing. But you know what? Nothing is more important than taking care of yourself and taking care of your health. That's the most valuable lesson that fitness has taught me.

▶ **Build variety into your fitness program.** People who really integrate exercise into their lives rarely do only one sport. It's simply more fun and interesting, and actually better for your body, to do two or three different kinds of exercise each week. If you live in a place that has seasonal changes, changing exercises with the seasons can be a good way to change your routine. Try to do various exercises for your cardiovascular system, strength and flexibility. See the following chapter, **Understanding Fitness**, for more information on how to cross-train.

▶ **Surround yourself with people whose goals are like your own.** It's going to be very difficult sticking to an exercise program if you hang around with a lot of beer-drinking, potato-chip-eating "couch potatoes." It's very helpful to be around people who are not only supportive of what you are doing, but are also committed to their own positive growth and fitness success.

> *Nothing is more important than taking care of yourself and taking care of your health.*

We are social animals and we tend to gravitate toward the people and situations that make us comfortable. If you are starting to get your body in motion, it's good to open up to people like yourself, or even those who are at a higher level than you are. I've found that most of the time,

people can't wait to share their knowledge, if you only dare to ask.

▶ **See yourself achieving your goal.** Employ imagery and visualization to picture yourself obtaining your goal. Visualizing your goal simply means creating a mental photograph of what you want to look like, how you want to feel, or what you want to be doing. You carry that photograph in your mind and you can look at it any time you want to.

Visualization works because it helps to reinforce the behaviors that will get you where you want to be. If you visualize yourself using perfect form to shoot perfect free-throws in basketball, your mind will remember this practice and instruct your body to do it on the court. If you visualize yourself losing body fat as you eat healthy foods and exercise, your mind will instruct your body to follow the behavior that reinforces this goal.

Visualization, when done with great concentration, can be almost as useful as actual practice in terms of improving sports performance. If you want to enter your first triathlon, visualize yourself pushing through the finish line on race day, feeling strong and exhilarated. If your goal is to get a muscular, lean body, take a look in the mirror and with your mind, draw in the muscles.

Visualization provides strong reinforcement to the brain to guide our behavior toward the goals we want to achieve.

▶ **Share the wealth.** Finally, share your new-found fitness knowledge with someone else. This is a guaranteed way to make you feel good about yourself, as well as a good way to do someone else a favor. Teaching someone else the benefits of exercise will remind you of the steps you've taken to get where you are, and will reinforce how positive your behavior has been. I can't tell you how many aerobics instructors I know who were once the unfit and uncoordinated student at the back of the class. Now they are in terrific shape and they are the greatest motivators.

But then, fitness is like that. It's such a good feeling that people want to spread it around.

Off Days

Over a period of time, you're going to have "off" days. Everyone has them—even the most advanced and well-trained athletes. On these days, it's good to do your program anyway, but ease off a little to adjust to whatever is happening to you.

Just the other day I went on my run which usually takes me about 30 minutes. Just after starting, I knew it was not my day. In fact, this feeling started earlier that day. I thought, "This is it. This is the day I'm going to quit in the middle and not finish my workout..." But before I gave up completely I decided to slow down a bit and try to continue. So I did... and then I had to slow down even more... I finally got to a jogging pace that was just slightly faster than my walking pace, and I managed to complete my usual distance.

Even though I finished the run in a time I could have beaten at age nine, I felt great for just finishing a run that is usually "no sweat" for me. A couple of days later, I ran the same course in a time that was close to my personal best.

Expect those "off days," and more importantly, accept them. And when you have an off day, remind yourself that it is better to do something than to do nothing at all.

If You're Very Unfit

If you're sixty years old and have never exercised, or if you are very overweight, or if you've never before started a fitness program, you may wonder if there is any point in starting now. Of course there is! In fact, the people who achieve the greatest and most noticeable benefits from exercise are those who have never exercised before! Many studies have proven that even people in their eighties and beyond can achieve significant physiological improvements—in muscle strength, bone mass, lowered body fat and cardiovascular health—by beginning an exercise program. Exercise does not discriminate. It's good for everyone!

Getting Started

Before beginning an exercise program, you may want to check with your doctor. This is especially true if you are over thirty-five, or if you have high blood pressure, diabetes or heart disease. If it's been so long since you've been to a doctor that you don't even know if you have any of these things, now might be a good time to go. Chances are your doctor will congratulate you for wanting to get out there and get your body in motion.

For Beginners: A Walking Program

The best place to start for beginners or people who haven't exercised in a while is with a simple, straightforward walking program. Walking is

Share your new-found fitness knowledge with someone else.

great for everyone—it costs nothing and requires no special equipment.

Begin by walking slowly for a few minutes, then gradually pick up your pace. Set an exercise time goal for yourself. A good starting rate, if you're not an exerciser, is 15 minutes of walking, three times a week. If you know this is too easy for you, start at 30 minutes, three times a week, or somewhere in between. After a few minutes at a slow pace as a warm-up, walk as briskly as possible. Be sure you are walking quickly enough so that you feel yourself breathing faster, but not so quickly that you cannot hold a conversation as you go. The "talk test" is a good check to see that you are working hard enough to receive cardiovascular benefits, but not so hard that you will tire too fast or get dizzy. For more information on measuring how hard you're exercising, see page 31.

Keep increasing the length of your walks as you progress. At first you will just increase the time it takes you to finish your walk, but as your fitness level increases you will find that you are covering more distance in a given period of time, because your pace will be increasing, too.

At some point in your walking routine, you may want to start jogging or slow running. It's up to you. You certainly don't have to progress to running—plenty of people stay very fit by vigorous walking programs alone. But if you do want to try jogging, work into it slowly and easily. Again, begin with a

> *Always walk away from your workout feeling like you have some energy left.*

warm-up of brisk walking, then start jogging when you feel ready. When you begin to tire or feel uncomfortable, slow to a fast walk again. When you've caught your breath, jog for a few more blocks. Keep alternating jogging and walking until you've completed your goal time—say 20 minutes to start. As your program continues, you will soon find yourself jogging more and walking less—and increasing your time to 30 minutes or more.

For more detailed information on beginning a walking or running program, see page 190.

Another good place for beginners to start is with a short-distance, flat bike ride or a relaxed swim. Both require more equipment than a walking program, but if they appeal more to you, do them. Remember that finding an exercise that is fun for you is the most important part of getting started.

You can also look for a beginner-level aerobics class at your local health club. Many people find that exercise classes are a great way to get motivated for fitness, because other people there are working hard, just like you are. If you are a beginner, though, BE SURE you are in a beginner class. Nothing discourages beginner-level exercisers more than starting out in an exercise class that is too advanced. Talk to the people who work at the front desk of your gym or aerobics studio. They can direct you to the class that is right for you. Then introduce yourself to your instructor and explain that you are a new student, so that your instructor is aware and can explain to you anything you need to know for class.

When you are just starting out, think of your program this way: "How much can I do and still have some energy left over?" My recommendation for anybody who is pursuing health and fitness is always to walk away from your workout feeling like you have some energy left. Never finish your workout feeling like you gave it all you've got. You will do that later on when you become more fit, and even then you will only "go for it all" once in a while.

Maintenance

Fitness is a journey, not a destination. Often people look at fitness as a purely goal-oriented activity—a way to lose weight and look better. That's a start. Your real goal, however, should be to make fitness a part of your life. The benefits of fitness, both physically and mentally, are enormous and ongoing. But, of course, there is no end point to fitness. It's a life-long pursuit, but that doesn't mean it's a jail sentence. In fact, quite the opposite is true, as any life-long exerciser will tell you. I hear it time and time again from people who exercise—they believe the benefits are so enormously rewarding, both physically and psychologically, that they wouldn't give up exercise for anything.

Once you've reached your initial goals, you will want to maintain your new healthy lifestyle, and you will probably have new goals you want to achieve. An easy way to stay on track is to keep a written list of the new lifestyle changes you want to maintain. Review it once a week or so and see if you are keeping up those new changes, or if you've been slipping back into old habits.

Remember, work patiently and progressively on one goal at a time. The take-home message is to avoid discouragement at all times—instead, encourage success. Tell yourself that you control your eating and exercise habits; they do not control you. All you have to do is figure out a plan that works for you.

Stress: The Enemy of our Motivation

In the battle to stay motivated toward living a fit and healthy life, we find ourselves having to face many and varied opponents.

Living in today's society is not easy. The pace of daily life is very fast. We are constantly called upon to meet new challenges in all aspects of our lives. People today are more goal-oriented then ever before, and the competition out there can be fierce.

Stress is everywhere. It starts with your alarm clock in the morning and it continues all the way through to the evening news. The truth is that there is really no way to get away from it. But we can learn to be aware of stress and see how it can block our natural flow of energy and interfere with our motivation. I find that most of the time we can take action and do something about it. Being able to cope with stress, just like maintaining a good eating and exercise program, takes a little know-how and a little discipline.

Many times, I store the stress from daily life as pent-up energy. A great way to channel this energy is to have something to do with it. Exercise is a great way to turn stress from a negative into a positive force. Imagine this: You are at the end of your day and you are on your way to your workout class. You're in a traffic jam and an angry driver is behind you, constantly honking his horn. Since you, too, have some pent-up energy, you'd really like to roll your window down and give him a piece of your mind, but you have something better to do— you have to get to your class. You can "save" your frustrations and let them motivate you in your exercise class.

You cannot avoid stress, but you can react to it in a positive way. You can channel your stress into positive action through exercise. If today wasn't the best day—you were criticized unfairly at work, you got caught in a bad traffic jam, you came home from work and realized you forgot to do an important errand—take a few deep breaths, put on your exercise shoes, and use your fitness program to blow off some steam. I guarantee you'll feel better—it works every time.

Positive Stress

Anger, frustration and anxiety have major effects on our overall fitness. All of us complain of too much stress in our lives. But what is stress? Stress is the body's response to any demand that is made on it. Demands can be physical, such as a workout or playing a sport, but more often the kind of demands that are placed on us are mental or emotional demands.

But don't forget that stress has a positive side. Stress, like pain, is not an enjoyable part of our lives, but it serves an important purpose. It alerts us to the fact that we must activate our defenses. It compels us to action, just as it compelled our ancient ancestors, who, when being chased by predators, could suddenly flee or fight, or somehow find a way to safety.

Challenges in our lives that lead to stress can also lead to better performance and a sense of accomplishment. When under stress, we find the physical and mental reserves necessary to tackle the job, finish the race or solve the problem. We need some

stress—it helps us handle the difficulties of everyday life—but we also need to minimize the stress in our lives and to learn to cope better with stress and anxiety. Learning to cope better is the key to achieving mental balance, which in turn leads us on our way to better health.

The Stress Response

What exactly happens to our bodies in a stressful situation? First, our brain assesses the situation and sends hormones into the bloodstream. The heart pumps more blood to the muscles, and the muscles prepare for action. The lungs push more oxygen into the body. Blood pressure rises and blood vessels change in size. Because the muscles need extra blood and oxygen, blood flow to the digestive system may be cut off. Digestion stops or slows.

We experience these bodily changes as shortness of breath, sudden alertness or even irritability or an upset stomach. When the stressful situation passes, our body releases a different set of hormones that have a calming effect.

The stress cycle is normal for the body, but when it is repeated too frequently and too intensely, it begins to affect our overall health. A body that is constantly subjected to stress will have higher blood pressure, tense muscles and digestive problems. Continual stress also taxes the immune system, so it becomes harder for us to fight off disease. Eventually, too much stress leads to illness and exhaustion.

The idea is to deal with stress before we hit the exhaustion stage. This requires either removing some of the stress from our lives, or finding a way to cope with it better.

Don't forget that stress has a positive side.

Coping with Stress

Coping with stress—controlling it—will have the same effect on you as learning to control your good eating habits or maintaining an exercise program. It will give you a feeling of success and accomplishment in all areas of your life.

Here are some suggestions to help you handle stress and keep you on a motivated path toward health and fitness:

▶Schedule time each day just for yourself. Put it on your calendar, just like you schedule your exercise time. In fact, a good time might be right before or right after your exercise time. But it doesn't matter when—just make sure you make the time for it. You may have just twenty free minutes, but use it for you. Read, think, meditate, relax, listen to music, or just close your eyes for a while. Tell your family or your roommates that you are not to be disturbed during this time.

▶Schedule time for recreation. People need to play, and often we forget just to take time for fun.

▶Don't submit to the "appeal" of caffeine, alcohol, cigarettes and sleeping pills when you are stressed. Any of these will affect your nervous system, and while giving you brief release from your stress, can be very damaging in the long term. In fact, the more your nervous system is tampered with, the greater your stress response will become. Your body actually becomes less able to deal with stress.

▶Try to avoid food when you feel stressed. The tendency for many people is to eat too much, or too much of the wrong things, when under stress. You want to eat when you feel calm and in control, and when your digestive system is functioning smoothly.

▶Fight off stress with exercise. Don't let a hard day keep you from heading to the gym or the track. Fifteen minutes into your workout, you will feel a lot better.

▶Get enough sleep. One of the best coping devices for stress is lots of rest, which can mean either simple quiet time or plain old sleep. I am often surprised at how many people I meet who say that they are tired all the time, and then tell me that they get only five or six hours of sleep each night. When I ask them if they've ever tried sleeping more, they tell me they don't think they need more.

Although in our modern society we seem to have made it into some sort of human weakness to take time for sleep, getting more sleep could be a great key to achieving fitness and better health. Although every person is different, most studies indicate that the average person needs between seven and eight hours of sleep per night.

In general, quality of sleep seems more important than quantity, however. If you are waking up every hour or so during the night because of noise or other disturbances, and you have trouble getting back to sleep, you are probably going to feel tired the next day even if you were in bed for nine hours the night before. Try to find a sleeping area in your home that is free of disturbances like light, noise and movement, so that you can get continual quality sleep.

Fifteen minutes into your workout, you will feel a lot better.

▶Manage your time. Don't fall into the trap of intending to do more than you possibly can each day, making promises and appointments that you can't possibly keep. You'll find yourself racing around during the day, making apologies to everyone for being late and not getting your work done on time. Overscheduling is a major source of stress. If you can't do it, don't say you can.

▶Change your responses to stressful situations. Why grow angry and honk your horn in traffic? It does not help the situation and it only further irritates you. Learn to express your frustration in constructive ways. Don't bottle it up, but don't fight against things that you can't change.

▶Diet, too, can contribute to or reduce our level of stress, depending on how we treat it. Many people do not realize that eating a cheeseburger and fries, washed down with a large sugary soft drink, actually causes an immediate stress response in the body. Not so if you have a light meal of easily digested complex carbohydrates, with a little low-fat protein thrown in. Carbohydrates actually cause a relaxation response in the body. See the chapter on **Nutrition** (pages 45-60) for more information on what to eat for a healthier lifestyle.

▶Watch out for overtraining. Hopefully you will never have to worry about overtraining, but unfortunately there are people who become so obsessed with exercising that they overtrain, and their athletic performance actually suffers because of it. Here are some of the warning signs of overtraining:

▶trouble sleeping
▶chronic fatigue
▶loss of motivation
▶low energy
▶stressed immune system
▶muscle soreness and weakness
▶elevated resting heart rate of 10% more than normal (5 beats or more)

If you ever find yourself overtraining, decrease the frequency, intensity and duration of your workouts. You might even want to take a break altogether from exercise for a week or so. If you've only been doing one form of exercise, this might be a good time to try something different, or switch to cross-training. If you continue to have a problem with overtraining, seek professional counseling.

The Pendulum

As we all know, life has its ups and downs. Nothing lasts forever. When you are "on a roll," it's not everlasting. When you're feeling frustrated or down, that, too, has an end. While there is no way to avoid life's ups and downs, there are certainly ways to keep your balance through the constant shifts.

Imagine the cycles of life as a pendulum that moves back and forth, from left to right, with the middle being the point of perfect balance. From physics, we know that the energy of the pendulum is always in flux. As the pendulum moves through its balance point, all its energy is being used to move it. As the pendulum reaches its highest point, it slows down and stops, but its energy is not lost, it is just being stored, and will soon be used to move the pendulum back in the other direction.

Change your responses to stressful situations.

Like the pendulum, the energy in our lives is always in flux. Sometimes there are negative forces in our lives—stresses, frustrations and tensions—that slow us down. The important thing to understand is that, like the pendulum, we can channel these forces to help get us moving in the right direction again. I find that through physical exercise, by getting our bodies in motion, we can channel the negative forces of our lives to move us in a positive direction again.

In order to be able to deal with the complexity of the world today, we must be in shape both physically and mentally, and we have to set time aside on a regular basis to do the activities that accommodate our physical and mental well-being. Physical activity on a regular basis can have a dramatic positive effect on our lives.

In order to be able to turn to our fitness program for support, we need to stay with it and, more importantly, stay motivated. Getting our bodies in motion and getting in shape is an important goal for everyone. Keeping your body in motion on a regular basis as you go through life is the real challenge.

Understanding Fitness

Gilad and his mother, Ora Janklowicz, take a walk in the beach park. Ora appears on the Bodies in Motion show regularly.

I t seems that everyone wants to be fit and in good shape. The past two decades have seen people paying more and more attention to health and fitness. We have finally realized the overwhelming benefits that attention to our health provides. But what does it mean to be fit?

Some people equate fitness with losing weight and being slim. But slim people can be unfit also. Other people equate fitness with lots of muscles. But muscular people, too, can be unfit. Some people think fitness means being able to do 100 push-ups or run a marathon or compete in athletic events.

What does it mean to be a fit person? It means that you possess each of the five components of fitness: cardiovascular fitness, muscle strength, muscular endurance, flexibility and low body fat.

The Five Components of Fitness

▶**Cardiovascular fitness** is the capacity of the heart and lung system to deliver oxygen to working muscles. It means that you can walk or run or do other aerobic activities for thirty minutes or more and not get out of breath.

Being a fit person means that you possess each of the five components of fitness.

▶**Muscular strength** is the amount of force a muscle can exert during contraction. Muscular strength allows you to perform everyday tasks like lifting and carrying heavy objects with ease.

▶**Muscular endurance** is the number of times that a muscle can repeatedly exert the same force without fatiguing. If you have muscular endurance, your legs don't get tired out when you go hiking, and your arm doesn't wear out from two sets of tennis.

▶**Flexibility** is the range of motion possible around a joint. With good flexibility, you can perform exercises comfortably and with a wide range of motion. Flexibility adds grace to your movements, and keeps your muscles relaxed while you are doing an activity.

▶**Low body fat** is the body composition of someone who has a greater amount of lean body mass (muscles, bones, nervous tissue, skin and organs) and a lower amount of body fat. You can always tell a person with low body fat—they don't have any "extras" like flabby hips and thighs or a "spare tire."

We will discuss each of these five fitness components in turn, but first we should note that all of them are of equal importance, and no one component should be emphasized over the others. You don't want to be aerobically fit but unable to carry a heavy suitcase, nor do you want to be a bodybuilder who can't pass a treadmill test. You don't want to be a solid long-distance runner with a "spare tire" around your middle, nor do you want to be a great racquetball player who can't bend from the hips or stretch your hamstrings.

Let's look at the five components of fitness and see what each brings to our total health and wellness.

Cardiovascular Fitness

The buzzword in cardiovascular fitness since the late 1970s has been "aerobics." When most people hear that word, they think of aerobic dance classes, but actually "aerobics" means any exercise that can increase cardiovascular fitness. This includes walking, running, cycling, swimming, rollerblading, rowing, cross-country skiing, and any other sport that gets your heart beating faster and your lungs pumping air.

The amount of time it takes to achieve basic cardiovascular fitness is minimal. A half-hour, three or four days a week, can do it. Cardiovascular fitness means going after one goal: increasing your aerobic capacity. Your aerobic capacity is the maximum amount of oxygen that your body can process within a given time. That processing consists of your lungs taking in large amounts of oxygen from the air around you, and your vascular system circulating large volumes of blood and delivering the oxygen to all the parts of the body. What you want to do is increase your body's ability to do these tasks. This requires strong lungs and a healthy heart and vascular system (the arteries and veins that carry blood).

Aerobic Exercise Improves Cardiovascular Fitness

To increase your aerobic capacity, you need to do aerobic exercise. Aerobic exercise is any activity that requires additional oxygen for prolonged periods of time, and hence places demands on the body to improve its capacity to process oxygen. The key to improving cardiovascular fitness through aerobic exercise is to consider three variables:

▶**Exercise intensity** (how hard to exercise)—Exercise intensity should be approximately 60% to 85% of maximum heart rate reserve, which can be determined by using heart-rate monitoring techniques, as explained on pages 30-32.

▶**Exercise duration** (how long to exercise)—Exercise duration may vary, but cardiovascular fitness is best achieved by a minimum of 30 minutes of aerobic exercise. If you are a beginner, you may not be able to do continuous exercise for 30 minutes. You should do whatever amount you can and slowly build up.

▶**Exercise frequency** (how often to exercise)—Exercise frequency should be a minimum of three times per week to achieve cardiovascular fitness.

Understanding Heart Rate Monitoring

In the past decade, heart rate monitoring as a way of determining exercise intensity has become a raging fad. Students in aerobics classes stop mid-way through class to count their pulse rates, stationary bicycles come equipped with heart rate monitors, and you can even buy expensive electronic tools to carry with you as you jog, just to be sure your heart is pumping at the right number of beats per minute.

The whole point of measuring your heart rate is to help you exercise at an intensity that is challenging to you, but not so hard that you exhaust yourself too quickly. If you're a beginning exerciser, you might feel comfortable exercising at about 60% of your maximum heart rate, while a more advanced

Cardiovascular fitness depends on exercise intensity, duration and frequency.

exerciser can probably exercise at the 85% level or higher.

Eventually, you want to push yourself to train at a higher percentage of your maximum heart rate. Exercising at 75% of your maximum heart rate will make you moderately aerobically fit, but for maximum aerobic fitness you will have to exercise at a higher heart rate. You would want to achieve maximum aerobic fitness if you were training for competitive sports such as long-distance cycling, running or swimming. Generally, this kind of fitness can only by achieved by exceeding your anaerobic threshold—by training at the highest end of your aerobic capacity or beyond.

Determining Your Maximum Heart Rate and Aerobic Training Range

The maximum heart rate is the maximum number of beats per minute (BPM) that the average heart can beat during exercise. Maximum heart rate changes with age. It is estimated that the maximum heart rate is highest (approximately 220 BPM) when we are children of age 10 or so, and falls off as we get older.

You can determine your current maximum heart rate simply by subtracting your age from 220. If you multiply that number—220 minus your age—by 60% and 85%, you will find your aerobic training range— 60% at the low end and 85% at the high end. For a workout that is aerobic in nature, you

Keep in mind that not all 40-year-olds have exactly the same maximum heart rate.

should try to keep your heart rate within your aerobic training range. In general, only highly trained athletes would train at much more than 85% of their maximum heart rate. (The 60% to 85% percent range is suggested because it is difficult for untrained athletes to maintain exercise at a higher rate than that. If you can, however, you should—remember that you always want to push yourself to your personal best. Some marathon runners can run at 90% of their maximum heart rate for more than two hours.)

Here's an example of an "average" 40-year-old beginning or intermediate exerciser trying to find his or her aerobic training range:

At 40 years old, the exerciser's maximum heart rate is 180 beats per minute. That's 220 - 40 = 180.

Now, if we multiply 180 by 60% and 85%, we find their aerobic training range.

$$180 \times 60\% = 108 \qquad 180 \times 85\% = 153$$

So, if you are 40 years old, you would want to have your heart beating between 108 and 153 beats per minute when you are doing an aerobic activity that lasts approximately 30 minutes or longer.

On page 31 you will find a heart rate chart that follows the calculations we've talked about. Keep in mind that these numbers are only approximations. For example, not all 40-year-olds have exactly the same maximum heart rate. Some people have a higher or lower maximum heart rate than what is "normal" for their age, so their training range will also differ. But in general, especially if you are a beginning or intermediate exerciser, target heart ranges are good guidelines to follow when you are exercising aerobically.

Target Heart Rates

Age	60%	75%	85%
20	120	150	170
25	117	147	166
30	114	143	162
35	111	139	157
40	108	135	153
45	105	131	149
50	102	127	145
55	99	124	140
60	96	120	136
65	93	117	132
70	90	112	128

Checking Your Training Heart Rate

Now that you know what your training rate *should* be, how do you determine what your heart rate actually is when you are exercising? All you need is a watch or clock with a second hand. Wait until you've been exercising for 10 to 15 minutes, so you are past the warm-up stage but not too far into the hardest part of the workout. Then, slow down a bit, and lightly press your index and middle fingers of one hand against either your radial or carotid artery. Your radial artery is on the inside of your wrist; your carotid artery is just below your lower jaw, on either side of your neck. (Most people can feel their pulse in their neck more easily than in their wrist—see which way is fastest and easiest for you.)

Now, looking at your second hand, count your pulse beats for 10 or 15 seconds. If you count for 10 seconds, multiply that number by six to find your number of beats per minute. If you count for 15 seconds, multiply that number by four. This is your training rate in beats per minute. Now, how does it compare to your training range?

One note about counting your pulse beats: Sometimes exercisers will count their beats for only six seconds, and then multiply by 10 to get their beats per minute. This six-second count is generally not recommended because there is such a large margin of error if the pulse is not counted correctly. On the other hand, counting beats for 15 seconds is a bit long for advanced exercisers, because a well-conditioned athlete's heart rate will actually start coming down in that time. This drop in heart rate is known as good "recovery" for the heart, and the more fit you are, the faster your heart rate will return to normal after exercise. For beginning and intermediate exercisers, either the 10 or 15 second heart rate count should be a good indicator.

Heart rate monitoring is useful and important, but keep in mind that it is not completely scientific. Not all of us are completely accurate at counting our pulse beats. Also, you have to keep in mind

> *The more fit you are, the faster your heart rate will return to normal after exercise.*

that as an exerciser, you are always going to be a little different from other exercisers your age. You're even going to be different than you were the last time you exercised, due to changes in how you feel, the weather, your level of stress, etc. That's why it's good to use the RANGE of the target heart range, instead of expecting to train at the same exact number of beats per minute every day. Always pay attention to how you feel.

Other Ways to Monitor Your Heart Rate

There are other ways to monitor your heart rate, and one that is growing in popularity is the Rating of Perceived Exertion or RPE. This perceived exertion test is increasingly used by exercise instructors because it trains exercisers to pay attention to their own bodies and how they feel while they are exercising.

Basically, you rate how hard you feel you are working according to the Perceived Exertion Scale of 1 to 10.

▶1—very light
▶2—light
▶3—moderate
▶4—somewhat hard
▶5—heavy
▶7—very heavy
▶10—extremely heavy

Remember—always pay attention to how you feel.

Generally, beginning exercisers want to feel like they are around 4 on the scale, while more advanced exercisers could work around 7 or higher.

The Rating of Perceived Exertion is useful, but requires some practice to be used effectively. If you've never exercised before, you may have difficulty determining where you are on the scale. With some use, however, this scale can be very effective in training you to pay attention to your own subjective feelings about how you are doing as you exercise. This is ultimately important, because only you know when you've had enough or when you can go a little harder.

You should also understand that it is okay to increase or decrease your effort according to how you feel in a specific workout. If you started out too fast and you are thinking, "that's it—I can't go on," just slow down for several minutes, catch your breath, then start working more intensely again. Keep in mind our previous discussion about how important it is to work within your own ability.

If you want a very simple rule of thumb for monitoring your exertion, take the "talk test." Whatever activity you are performing, you should never be so out of breath that you cannot comfortably say a sentence or two out loud while you do it.

Resting Heart Rate

One important time to monitor your heart rate is when you are resting. Your resting heart rate can be used as an index of your general level of aerobic fitness: the lower your resting heart rate, the more fit you are. Regular exercise is going to lower your resting heart rate, which will benefit you every time you are not at rest and your heart needs to pick up the pace. It's a good idea to know what your resting heart rate is now, because as you become more fit, your resting heart rate is going to drop, and that will mean that your heart can perform with less effort.

The best time to measure your resting heart rate is when you first wake up in the morning, before getting out of bed. This is the ideal time both because you are fully rested and because you have not recently had a meal, which can raise your heart rate. Look at a clock with a second hand, and count the beats at your wrist or neck for a full 30 seconds, and then multiply by two. That number is your resting heart rate.

Your resting heart rate can be an excellent indicator of your overall well-being. An athlete who trains vigorously several days a week will check his or her resting heart rate very often, and generally will find it consistent within a beat or two. However, if your resting heart rate is elevated more than five beats above what is normal for you, it is often an indication of illness or stress, and can even indicate overtraining. Days when you have an unusually high resting heart rate are usually good days to slow down and train a little easier.

Try keeping a record of your resting heart rate throughout your exercise program. Most people who begin regular exercise programs will see a drop in their resting heart rates within a month or two. Marathon runners frequently have resting heart rates in the 50s or lower. More "normal" rates are in the 70s and 80s, but a better-than-average fit person will usually have a resting heart rate of between 50 and 70 beats per minute.

When I'm in really super shape, my resting heart rate can get as low as 42 to 44 beats per minute, and I'm not a long-distance runner. I achieve that level of cardiovascular fitness through a combination of two to three moderate runs per week of three to six miles per run, a few aerobics classes, a couple of speed training sessions on the track, and a moderate weight training program.

To improve your cardiovascular fitness, do any of the following aerobic workouts in this book: low or high impact aerobics (page 75), walk-ing/running/sprinting (page 189), or swimming and water aerobics (page 201).

Muscular Strength

People are starting to realize that aerobic exercise, while great for the heart and lungs and terrific for overall general health, is not an all-inclusive recipe for fitness. Possessing muscular strength is equally important, and actually provides many of the same benefits as cardiovascular fitness, such as lower blood pressure, lower resting heart rate, improvements in cholesterol levels, and lower body fat.

Muscular strength exercises are the fastest and quickest way to reshape, build, strengthen and tighten all the major muscle groups of the body, helping you get that fit and lean look. These types of exercises are very effective in improving your overall appearance and posture as well as increasing bone mass, which means a lower risk of diseases like osteoporosis. Having muscular strength also increases the strength of joints, therefore decreasing the risk of injury.

In fact, muscular strength is now recognized by the American College of Sports Medicine as a critical element of any exercise routine designed to promote overall good health. In 1990, the ACSM revised its long-standing exercise recommendations for overall fitness to include "strength training of moderate intensity at a minimum of two times

Your resting heart rate is an excellent indicator of your overall well-being.

per week," in addition to aerobic exercise three times a week.

How to Get Strong

Muscular strength can be improved by the use of free weights, weight machines, special rubberbands or other resistance devices, or by doing conditioning workouts such as the ones in this book (page 121). It is helpful to understand that improving your muscular strength will generally improve your muscular endurance as well (see next page). Muscular strength can be improved by progressive overload of the muscles, or continually challenging your muscles with greater amounts of weight or resistance.

Many people shy away from weightlifting because they think it will give them large, bulky muscles like the kind you see in bodybuilding magazines. Many women especially steer clear of the free weights in the gym for this reason. But it's important to know that with weight training, you can shape your muscles any way you want. You will only get big, bulky muscles if you lift extremely heavy weights in a very rigorous training program. But if you'd prefer toned, tight, smaller muscles, those can be attained by a weight training program such as the one in this book.

With weight training, you can shape your muscles any way you want.

In this program, you'll be lifting weights, but not extremely heavy weights. What's heavy for you can be determined with a little experimentation. You'll need to try differ-

ent size weights for each separate weight lifting exercise until you find a weight that you can lift approximately 12 times without exhaustion, with good form and without rest between repetitions. For every exercise you do, that weight amount is going to be different, so this takes some trial and error.

I suggest you always go for a lighter weight rather than a heavier weight at first. In my training, I do three sets per exercise, on the average. The first set is always my warm-up set (even though I've already completed my ten-minute general warm-up before touching a weight) and I perform 12 to 15 repetitions or "reps" in this set. My second set is my working set. I pick up a heavier weight than the warm-up set and try to do ten repetitions. My third set is my challenge set, and I try to perform seven to eight repetitions on this set.

So, just like in my routine, you want to form a pyramid with your three weightlifting sets:

heaviest - 8 reps

heavy - 10 reps

lightest - 12 reps

The most important element in weight training is maintaining correct posture and good strict form in your movement, so that only the muscles that you are working are contracting. If the weight you are using causes you to compromise your form, it is too heavy. Never work your muscles beyond their ability to train with perfect form. The main problems to watch out for in all exercises are the locking of joints, arching of the lower back, and jerking and fast movements.

Strength training is about control. Control the speed of the workout; control your posture and the resistance. You should use resistance you can control, not resistance that will control you.

Benefits of Strength Training

So now you can lift weights. What good will that do? Well, for starters, your strength is not the only thing that will improve. Your body is going to look different as well. Your body fat will drop, and you'll increase your lean muscle mass, so you'll have a longer, leaner look. Also, your chest, back, abdominals, arms and legs will become stronger. Your posture will improve, your bone mass will increase, your resting heart rate will probably drop, and you'll decrease your risk of injury to your joints and bones. Not too bad for a little weight training two or three times a week, and you can do it in as little as 30 to 45 minutes per workout.

If you want to get strong, turn to the conditioning workouts on page 121 or the weightlifting workouts on page 157.

Muscular Endurance

Muscular endurance is the length of time or number of times a muscle can exert force without fatiguing. It is sustained activity at below-maximal effort, unlike muscular strength which is brief activity at maximal or close to maximal effort.

Muscular endurance can be improved by using lighter weights or resistance than you would use for increasing muscular strength, and increasing the number of repetitions to 15 to 30 repetitions per set. Muscular endurance can also be improved by playing sports which require the repetitive force of certain muscles.

How many push-ups can you do consecutively, with good form, before reaching exhaustion? This is a muscular endurance exercise. To improve your push-up muscular endurance, you have to spend time doing push-ups. Also, any strength-training exercise that you do for the chest and shoulders is going to improve your muscular endurance in push-ups.

Your muscular strength exercise regimen in the gym can easily be converted into a muscular endurance training session by simply lowering the weights to a level where you can do 20 to 30 repetitions per exercise.

With endurance training exercises, just as with strength training exercises, you want to do three sets. The first set is a warmup set (try to do at least 25 to 30 repetitions of an exercise). Set two is the working set (try to do 20 to 25 repetitions). Set three is the challenge set—the set in which you try to go for that "extra" push, without compromising your form, of course. You should do 15 to 20 repetitions in this final set. You can either keep the same amount of weight in all three sets, or increase the weight just a little in each successive set.

If you want to work on your muscular endurance, do the conditioning workouts on page 121 or the weightlifting workouts on page 157. Just be sure to modify the weight and number of repetitions so that you are lifting less weight with more repetitions per set as discussed above.

Flexibility

This is one component of fitness that a lot of regular exercisers overlook or don't spend enough time doing. Ironically, it can be one of the most enjoyable elements of a workout! Most people I know finish their workout and off they go, with-

> *To improve your push-up muscular endurance, you have to spend time doing push-ups.*

out a proper cool-down and stretch. Stretching, or working on flexibility, is immensely helpful in maintaining fitness. Increased flexibility will help you reduce your risk of injury and increase the range of motion of your joints.

Stretching regularly will definitely lengthen your athletic career, by helping muscles and joints stay flexible and workable, and by helping to prevent debilitating muscle and joint injuries. Stretching and relaxation exercises will also help reduce the recovery period between workouts.

How to Stretch

Some people are more flexible than others. While much of flexibility depends on genetics, anyone can improve their flexibility through proper stretching. Proper stretching means stretching when the muscles are warm, such as toward the end of a warm-up, or at the very end of a workout. Cold muscles and tendons do not have enough elasticity to be stretched—they must be warmed first.

Proper stretching also means static stretching—holding each stretch for 10 to 30 seconds. Avoid any bouncing movement when you stretch. Although you will sometimes see people do it, there should be no bouncing or ballistic movements in stretching, as these moves can actually cause tiny tears in the muscles being stretched.

Stretching regularly will definitely lengthen your athletic career.

Stretching should never involve any pain, even if you are very inflexible. The most important part

of flexibility training is stretching each muscle within the limits of comfort. Forcing a stretch, or overstretching a muscle beyond what it can comfortably do, actually causes the muscle to contract in order to protect itself from being torn. This is the reverse of what you want to achieve—you want the muscle to expand, lengthen and relax in a stretch.

Pay attention to your breathing as you stretch. Don't hold your breath. If you exhale and inhale rhythmically, trying to relax into the stretch, you will stretch deeper and further. Move gently from one stretch to the next—make no jerking movements. The whole process of stretching is slow and relaxed. That's what makes it so great to do after a workout, or just after a hard day.

I suggest that you do three sets of any given stretch. In the first set, you get into position, making sure you are maintaining good posture, and try to feel your range of movement by slowly breathing out. Then relax and let go of the stretch.

In the second set, start by taking a couple of deep breaths, and then on the third breath, slowly exhale and get back into position, trying to go a little further this time without feeling tense and uncomfortable. Keep breathing and reaching into the stretch. As you exhale, try to let all the tension in your body dissolve. Let go of the stretch and gently "shake out" the area being stretched.

In the third set, repeat what you did on set two, and try to go just a bit further, still maintaining a relaxed posture throughout the whole stretch. Remember, you are stretching to the point of your own limitation and not to the point of pain.

How Often to Stretch

Keep in mind that flexibility is often one of the most difficult components of fitness to achieve. No one becomes flexible overnight. It is a slow process, especially if you haven't done much stretching previously. One of the greatest things about stretching is that it is a relaxation exercise and doesn't require a lot of effort, so it can be done almost daily, even on days when you are ill or otherwise unable to exercise. (Just be sure to do a short warm-up first to prepare the body for stretching.) And it takes very little time to stretch each of the major muscle groups of the body. The more often you do it, the more flexible you will become. I recommend that no matter what your level of fitness, you should spend five to ten minutes stretching three to five days a week.

To improve your flexibility, do the cool-down routine on page 97 and the progressive flexibility routine on page 109.

Lowering Your Body Fat

Take two people of the same height, same body type and same frame. One appears lean and fit; the other appears overweight and out of shape. If you put them both on the scale, you'll find that the person who looks overweight and out of shape weighs the same or even less than the person who is lean and fit.

What's happening here? Since muscle is two and a half times heavier than fat, the answer is very simple, and it ties in to both exercise and nutrition habits. When you exercise on a regular basis and eat a healthy diet, you are constantly challenging your muscles to perform, causing them to get stronger and more dense and to weigh more. At the same time, you are burning off fat. In other words, you are turning your body into a lean and healthy machine. You are gaining muscle weight and you are losing body fat. People who are very muscular can weigh more than people of the same height who are sedentary, but have much slimmer figures and wear smaller-sized clothes.

If You Must Check the Scale

Because of the density of muscle, I don't see much point in having fit people weigh themselves as an indicator of their body fat. If you're one of those people who feel they have to get on the scale, however, there are a few simple formulas for determining what your approximate weight should be if you are a reasonably fit, exercising person. One formula that I think is fairly accurate is this one:

If you are a man, you should weigh 106 pounds for your first five feet of height. After the first five feet, every inch should weigh another six pounds. So, if you're a man who stands five feet, nine inches tall, you should weigh approximately 160 pounds. That's 106 + (9 x 6) = 160.

If you're a woman, you should weigh 100 pounds for your first five feet of height, and then five pounds for every inch over five feet. So, if you're a woman who is five feet, five inches tall, you should weigh approximately 125 pounds. That's 100 + (5 x 5) = 125.

Remember, these are just approximations, which don't take into account factors like your frame size or exact level of muscularity.

When you exercise and eat a healthy diet, you are turning your body into a lean and healthy machine.

Getting Your Body Fat Measured

If you believe you are not lean enough, or that you have "weight" to lose, you may want to get your body fat tested. That is the surest way to know if you are overfat, which is far more important than the number your scale registers.

You can find out your percentage of body fat by being weighed under water (hydrostatic weighing) or by using skinfold calipers. Most hospitals, sports medicine clinics, and many health clubs perform skinfold caliper body fat testing, in which the skin is "pinched" between calipers and measured. It is very important, however, that the technician using the calipers knows what he or she is doing—it is easy to get a misreading if it is not done correctly. You might want to have your caliper test done twice, by two different people. Hydrostatic weighing, where your underwater weight is compared to your dry-land weight to determine body density, is a more accurate method of measuring body fat.

What's a Reasonable Body Fat Level?

Most women have somewhere between 15 and 38 percent body fat. They *should* have approximately 15 to 25 percent body fat. (Marathon runners and other advanced athletes may have lower percentages.)

Most men average between 12 and 24 percent body fat. Men *should* have approxi-

A low-fat, nutritious diet, plus regular exercise, equals a lean body.

mately 10 to 19 percent body fat. Physically fit men may go as low as 6 to 12 percent.

How to Do It

So how do you become lean and fit, with a low percentage of body fat? The answer is very simple and it has two parts. You've heard it many times before—the answer is diet and exercise. A low-fat, nutritious diet, plus regular exercise, equals a lean body.

I repeat this well-known formula only because I know that there are still many people out there who are employing only one of the two parts of the equation, seeking a quick fix or a shortcut on their way to their desired weight. Or they are impatient and try to do it all at once, only to find discouragement and disappointment. When it comes to health and fitness, there are no quick fixes and solutions. Those who fall into those traps end up going in and out of shape and losing and gaining weight over and over again.

Neither component—diet nor exercise—is really effective over the long term without the other. People who go on strict diets to lose weight but don't work out will probably lose some weight, but they will lose both muscle and fat. They will probably still be unhappy with how they look.

And people who start exercising but don't cut back on the fat in their diets also have a hard time achieving a low body fat ratio. If you walk two miles in 30 minutes, you'll burn up around 200 calories, depending on your weight and fitness level. And if you run three miles in 30 minutes, you'll burn up about 350 calories. The fact is, though, the body needs to burn 3,500 calories to lose one pound of weight. That's going to be a lot of running or walking! If you exercise a lot, but don't cut the fat out of your diet, you'll get stronger but you won't decrease your body fat level nearly as dramatically as you would by eating properly as well.

Another important point to understand about dieting for weight loss is that if you once lost weight by only counting calories, and then one day try this same technique again, it will be much harder to do the second time. Why? Simply because you've trained your body to react to what it perceives as "starvation," a sudden decrease in the number of calories it gets each day. Our very clever bodies don't like that, and they respond by activating their "starvation response," which lowers the metabolic rate, requires less food, and stores whatever food it can get as fat. So, by repeatedly following low-calorie diets, you are teaching your body how to better store food as fat.

What you want to do instead is alter your fat to muscle ratio, so you get more active muscle tissue busily burning calories in your body. Muscle tissue, unlike fat, actually burns calories *while at rest*. This means that increased muscle mass actually raises your metabolic rate so you can become a lean, calorie-burning machine, instead of a non-active and defensive body expecting starvation at every turn.

Therefore, the solution for getting rid of excess body fat is simple—diet and exercise. And when I say "diet," I don't mean some depriving eating plan that makes you examine your food intake as a potential mathematical riddle filled with equations of calorie counts or calories burned per minute of activity. My idea of a proper diet is simply nutritious and healthy eating (see the following chapter on **Nutrition**). As for exercise, the best exercise for fat loss is a combination of exercise, especially any exercise that includes aerobics *and* weight training.

Different Types of Exercise— Crosstraining

We've discussed the five components of fitness—cardiovascular exercise, muscular strength, muscular endurance, flexibility and low body fat. The key to improving overall health and fitness is finding a balanced workout program that will target all five components.

One of the best ways to achieve balance in your exercise program is to cross train—vary your exercise program with different activities. We've all heard about cross training. Athletic shoe companies are doing their best to make us believe that cross training is a brand new workout concept that they've just invented, but the truth is that cross training, or variety training or split training or whatever else it is called, has been around as long as athletes have been around. The bottom line is that this concept really works, and it works for everyone.

My own personal exercise regimen involves quite a lot of cross training. I vary my program all the time. For instance, I'll combine both long distance and short distance running. I'll swim in the ocean, of course. (Living in Hawaii is like having a pool right at your doorstep.) Occasionally I'll play soccer or do other sports activities like scuba diving. I'll strength train with weights on the average of three times per week, and of course I teach aerobic exercise classes.

One of the best ways to achieve balance in your exercise program is to cross train.

I go through different phases. Recently, I competed in the Aloha Games, a sort of mini-Olympics designed for Hawaiian residents. It is open to the public and divided into age groups. My goal was to compete in the short distance runs, like the 100-meter dash. So for several months prior to the event, I concentrated more on speedwork and short distance runs, gave up some of my long-distance running, and lightened up a bit on my strength training too.

At another time, I picked up scuba diving as a sports hobby, so I found myself spending more time swimming in the ocean.

Now, as I'm working on this book, I've taken on the triathlon. I've never done a triathlon before, and I've never been very good at endurance events. But I thought I'd give it a shot. It will give me a chance to improve my endurance in a fun yet challenging way.

I find that cross training is the best way to balance a good workout program. It eliminates the typical "burnout" or "boredom" syndrome of doing one single activity over and over. It's more versatile and therefore easier for anyone with a busy schedule. It keeps your fitness activities more healthy, fun, and alive, and allows your body more rest between repetitions of the same activity.

Ideally, you want to choose activities in your cross-training program so that in the course of one week you'll address all five components of fitness. You'll find that even if you love one specific sport—be it playing softball or jazz dancing or whatever you do as a hobby—getting involved in a basic cross training program will greatly enhance your performance in your specific sport.

Even if you do only two sports—say you play softball on the weekend and you run twice a week—you are already doing a basic cross training workout. Now if you add two workouts per week in the gym for strength training, and on one of those days you also incorporate a bike ride (stationary or outdoor) or an aerobics class, you are really on the crosstraining road!

Your program can and should change from time to time based on your goals. The beauty of cross training is that you can tailor your program to your changing needs and goals. If your goal is, for example, track running, your focus would be on three to four track workouts per week and you would supplement these workouts with either swimming, weight lifting, an aerobics class or a long distance run.

The following page shows some sample cross training routines designed for the beginner, intermediate and advanced exerciser interested in achieving general overall fitness, using the workouts in the second half of this book.

> *The beauty of cross training is that you can tailor your program to your changing needs and goals.*

Beginning Cross Training Program

Monday
Walking program Phase I
Cool down and stretch

Tuesday
Swimming workout—beginner level

Wednesday
Walking program Phase I

Thursday
Rest

Friday
Walking program Phase I
Progressive flexibility training

Saturday
Low impact aerobics
Conditioning workout #1

Sunday
Rest

Intermediate Cross Training Program

Monday
Running program Phase I

Tuesday
Weightlifting workout #1
Progressive flexibility training

Wednesday
Running program Phase I

Thursday
Weightlifting workout #2
Progressive flexibility training

Friday
High impact aerobics
Water aerobics & conditioning

Saturday
Running program Phase I

Sunday
Rest

Advanced Cross Training Program

Monday
Weightlifting workout #1
Long distance run
Progressive flexibility training

Tuesday
Weightlifting workout #2
Swimming workout—advanced

Wednesday
Long distance run
Speed workout #1
Progressive flexibility training

Thursday
Weightlifting workout #1
Water aerobics & conditioning

Friday
Conditioning workout #2
Long distance run

Saturday
Low impact aerobics
Speed workout #2
Progressive flexibility training

Sunday
Rest

▶Notice that the cardiovascular element is the one element that is repeated at least three times a week. As we learned in the section on cardiovascular fitness, aerobic exercise must be performed three times a week for a minimum of 30 minutes to be effective in training the heart and vascular system.

Weight training or resistance training (including calisthenics) should be performed at least twice a week, preferably three times.

▶Also note that I did not mention any exercises that are specifically designed for the fifth component of fitness: low body fat. That's because any exercise you do will help you achieve lowered body fat, when combined with a nutritious low-fat diet. In fact, the best way to lower your body fat is to combine various types of exercise, especially aerobics and strength training, with a low-fat diet.

How Much and How Often

No matter what kind of training you do, I recommend you do something at least three times a week. If your fitness level is high enough, you should be exercising more often—maybe five or six times a week. But I do believe that everyone should take at least one day a week off from any exercise program. One day of complete rest for the body will vastly improve your performance on the other six days.

Also, if you are exercising more than every other day, I recommend that you alternate heavy workout and light workout days. For instance, if you are exercising five days a week, every weekday, you might want to have a hard workout on Monday, Wednesday and Friday (a long or fast run, for instance) and then a lighter workout on Tuesday and Thursday (a shorter jog or cycling or an aerobics class). Going all-out several days in a row is going to cause burn-out, and quite possibly injury.

The best way to lower your body fat is to combine aerobics and strength training with a low-fat diet.

Remember, heavy and light workouts are just changes in intensity or duration. A run can be both a heavy and a light workout, but the "light" run might be at a slower pace or for a shorter distance.

Training Methodology

How fast will you get to the goal you set for yourself? If you are committed to a program and really work at it, you can achieve noticeable results in six short weeks, good results in twelve weeks and excellent results in six months.

The most important thing to remember is to let go of the idea that you can accomplish your goal faster if you take a short cut such as a crash diet or working twice as hard as your body can handle in its present condition. In fact, those are two sure ways to put you right into the "roller coaster" club of those who gain, lose, gain, lose and so on.

The fact is, if you work within your ability and if you implement slow and controlled changes that your body can adapt to, those changes will become comfortable and permanent and you will achieve incredible results.

Your fitness program should include three phases:

Short term

4 to 8 weeks

This is the precondition phase. You condition yourself to get used to a workout program and to be able to do the training required. This is the part of the workout when you are building the foundation—you are logging workout time. You should be working at only 40 to 50% of your ability, even if you feel you can do more. This will ensure that you start a process of building up, rather than breaking down.

Mid term

4 to 8 weeks

This is the period in which you start increasing the pace of your workout and "thickening" the program by adding an extra workout or another cross training activity. This is the time to increase the volume and shorten the recovery periods of your workouts. During this phase, work at 50 to 70% of your ability.

Long term

for life

In this phase, you prepare to meet the goal that you set for yourself. Now that you've built a foundation and have a solid track record, you can start doing what you initially set out to do. This is also a base from which you can go on to even greater improvement. At this phase of the workout, you can start pushing to 70% effort and beyond on a regular basis.

By following the three phases in your various programs, you will:

▶Help prevent injuries
▶Keep from overtraining
▶Develop confidence and a positive attitude toward your training
▶Build your body up rather than break it down

How to Know If You're Getting More Fit

There are several factors to look for to see if your fitness level is improving. Often when you are in the middle of something, it is difficult to see the small changes that are occurring and pushing you closer to your goal. That's why record-keeping can really help you—you'll have written proof of the improvements that are happening. Keep a small notebook with records of your exercise sessions. Include facts like when you exercised, for how long, what you did, how far you went, how fast, how you felt, how much weight you lifted and how many times, what stretching exercises you did, etc. Or you can photocopy the Personal Profile chart on the following page and use it to chart your progress.

Also, look for the following signs of improvement:

▶Increase in endurance—ability to train for a longer period of time without becoming exhausted.

▶Increase in strength—ability to lift more weight or perform more repetitions than previously, without becoming exhausted.

▶Increase in flexibility—ability to perform muscle stretching exercises with more flexibility than before.

▶Decrease in body fat—a leaner look to your body: previous areas of fat deposits (such as "love-handles," thighs, buttocks) shrinking and muscle beginning to show through.

▶Improvement in appearance and health—you'll feel it and know it. It's an unmistakable feeling.

> *Let go of the idea that you can accomplish your goal faster if you take a short cut.*

PERSONAL PROFILE

WEEK NUMBER: _____

AGE: _____

WEIGHT: _____

BODY FAT %: _____

RESTING PULSE RATE: _____

SPEED:

    40 YARD DASH _____

    100 YARD DASH _____

STRENGTH:

    BENCH PRESS _____

    SQUAT _____

    SIT UPS per minute_____

ENDURANCE:

    1 MILE RUN _____

    5 MILE RUN _____

Nutrition:
The Basics

The human body is a very delicate and intricate machine, and food is its essential fuel. Food is the energy that powers our bodies and it is largely responsible for how we feel each day. Becoming aware of that fact can help you to appreciate what you put in your body, to make more discriminating choices, and also to enjoy eating. In a fast-paced society where processed foods are abundant, it is difficult to get proper nutrition unless you develop an awareness of what is good for you and what isn't. You must be willing to pay attention to what you put into your body.

A lot of advertising and marketing techniques are directed at our weaknesses. We see so many commercials on TV and in magazines that advertise fast foods, sugar, cigarettes and alcoholic drinks. They show beautiful people with beautiful bodies, photographed in exotic locations, holding in their hands cans of....you know the rest.

What's wrong with this picture? Well, the ads are not telling the whole truth. I doubt that those beautiful bodies regularly eat and drink what they are advertising. They are professional models and they get paid to glamorize the consumption of certain products. You'll never see an ad showing an intoxicated driver coming out of his wrecked car, holding his favorite beer can in his hand, telling you to GO FOR IT!

Nor would you see a commercial showing a hospital patient suffering from heart problems

> *The human body is a very delicate and intricate machine, and food is its essential fuel.*

and high blood pressure glancing through his favorite fast food menu and telling you to eat foods that are high in fat and salt. Unfortunately, these types of ads would be a little more realistic.

The bottom line is that we need to become more aware of what we are putting in our bodies. We don't have to be influenced by food manufacturers and advertising agencies. Let's get off the "see-food" diets; we don't have to eat everything we see.

Let's talk about diets. When I say "diet," I'm not talking about a low-calorie weight loss spree. I'm referring to your daily intake of food, whether it's "good food" or "bad food." The only way to start eating in a way that supports a fit lifestyle is to start thinking about your food in a healthy way. Often we will eat "bad" foods when we are upset, angry or anxious. Many people find relief in sweets or alcoholic beverages. It's a temporary escape—a momentary consolation for our emotional state.

You need to become aware of what you are eating. Eating healthily, once you are aware of it, is actually an easier way to eat, because you simplify your diet. You begin to eat more whole foods in their natural state, rather than processed foods. As you simplify your diet and eat more naturally, you will also start regulating your meals, cutting down on unhealthy in-between snacks, and becoming aware of artificially-produced products. Once you start eating healthier, you'll feel the change and you'll get addicted to this good feeling.

I know many people who exercise regularly and with plenty of enthusiasm. But when it comes to their diet, well, that's another story. You shouldn't look at your exercise program as a way to burn off bad eating habits. I'm not trying to preach to you to restrict your diet to the point of boredom, but it is better to develop good daily eating habits so when you feel like letting go once in a while, you'll have a great place to come back to. Keep in mind that just as you can exercise your body into good shape, you can also exercise your taste buds into good shape.

Personally, over the years I've improved my own diet tremendously as I've become more aware of how much better I perform in sports and how much better I feel when I eat healthily. I used to hate vegetables and I never ate much fruit. I got my sugar in the form of ice cream. I didn't know the important role that carbohydrates play in fueling my body.

In the last ten years, through reading, learning, talking to experts, and through experimenting with what I eat, I've learned the importance of a well-balanced diet. I eat vegetables and fruit often, and I eat the right ratio of protein and carbohydrates. I try to eliminate excess fat wherever I can in my diet. The main difference between how I feel today compared to how I felt years ago is that now I have a lot more energy and vitality.

I've noticed that when you eat the right things over a period of time, you lose the cravings that usually accompany unhealthy diets. I still feel I'd like to have a certain food every once in a while, but I have a lot more control over this feeling simply because I give my body all the main natural foods it needs most of the time. My emphasis now is on basic nutrition—eating foods that make me feel healthy. And that is the goal—to make healthy choices as often as you can.

A Few Words About Diets

A "diet" is something that people go on with the hope of losing weight. A "diet" is usually not a life-long commitment or choice; it is conceived and accomplished with a very short-term goal in mind: lowering the number on the scale. The word "diet" conjures images of us depriving ourselves of the foods we enjoy. The word "diet" is actually going out of fashion as more and more nutritionists, psychologists, athletic trainers, and others who are interested in what we eat promote the idea that dieting is not good for us, neither mentally nor physically.

Instead, they say, we need to become "natural eaters," who eat to supply our bodies with the fuel we need to live each day. Natural eaters concern themselves with what food will energize and sustain them. Natural eaters eat only until they are satisfied, never any more or any less. Natural eaters are aware of what foods are good for them, but they are not obsessive about calorie counting or eating exact amounts or types of food.

Natural eating is instinctual. It is only through the process of socialization that we end up confusing other issues with eating, and forget our natural ability to choose the right food for us. So we learn to like sweets, because our parents gave them to us as a reward when they were happy with us. We learn to enjoy processed foods, because that is what is readily available. We develop a fondness for salt and fat—because that is what much of our processed food consists of.

Diet Policy

The key policy on diets is this: Don't even think about going on any

> *When you eat the right things over a period of time, you lose the cravings that usually accompany bad diets.*

diet that you wouldn't want to stay on for the rest of your life. A diet should never be a temporary fix—it should be a lifelong eating pattern that emphasizes balanced nutrition. Remember: what you want to develop are good eating habits that will last a lifetime. At no point in this book will I tell you that you have to cut out every one of your favorite foods or go on some restrictive diet. That kind of thinking will not lead to long-term success, and we are in this for the long term.

In the previous chapter, I pointed out that there is not much point in being obsessed with the scale. Here, I'll say the same about calorie counting. If you eat good, healthy wholesome food that sustains your fit lifestyle, most of the time you need not worry about calorie counting. In fact, if you have to worry about how many calories are in something you want to eat, it probably doesn't belong in your diet.

Let's talk about nutrition. Making a commitment to eating nutritional foods is a far cry from putting yourself on a diet, and it will bring much better results without any deprivation. While dieting or denying yourself foods is a negative step, committing to eat nutritive foods is a positive step. Once the commitment to good eating is made, the benefits follow naturally and easily.

> *If you have to worry about how many calories are in a food, it probably doesn't belong in your diet.*

Benefits

Benefits of a nutrient-rich diet include lower body fat, greater energy, better-looking skin and hair, restful sleep, fewer digestive problems, a healthy-looking glow, and a wonderful sense of control in your life, because you are doing what you know is good for you. When you put good things inside of you, it starts to show on the outside.

Good nutrition is no secret. The popular media is loaded with information on how to eat healthfully. A healthy diet includes carbohydrates, protein and fat in the proper amounts and from proper sources. It is low in fat, salt, sugar, caffeine and alcohol.

However, despite the spotlight on nutrition in the past decade, many people still do not eat a healthy diet. In fact, the average American in the early 1990s is eating four times the amount of fat he or she needs, ten to fifteen times the sodium he or she needs, and nearly a third of a pound of sugar a day.

Seems almost impossible that we could be taking in all this bad food, right? Well, much of it is hidden in processed foods. If there is one change that you could make to your diet right now that would have the biggest impact on your overall health, it would be to eliminate or greatly reduce processed foods from your diet. Processed foods are those packaged foods we buy that are ground, bleached, fried, preserved, hydrogenated, or sweetened. They're so far removed from their natural state that they're not even really "food" any more.

A good rule of thumb is to eat foods that are as close to their natural state as possible. The natural state of fruit is whole, in its skin, not in a can with sugar or syrup added. The natural state of vegetables is raw, or very lightly cooked, not frozen with cream sauce poured over them. Grains are closest to their natural state as whole-grain breads, not as bleached-all-purpose-flour-based-with-fats-and-stabilizers-added white bread. And so on.

Let's take a closer look at the basic food groups we need:

Carbohydrates

Complex carbohydrates should make up the largest part of your diet—60 to 75 percent of your entire daily food intake. They are the long-term, sustaining fuel of the body, and when they are burned, they leave only water and carbon dioxide as end products. That makes complex carbohydrates very easy on the body's digestive system.

Carbohydrates are converted by the body into glucose, the form of sugar found in the bloodstream, which fuels the brain, the nervous system and the muscles. Although some glucose is stored in the muscles and liver as reserve fuel, too much excess glucose is stored by the body as fat.

Complex versus Simple Carbohydrates

When we discuss carbohydrates in this book, we are talking about complex carbohydrates only. Simple carbohydrates should be avoided—they are sugars that are converted too rapidly into glucose and absorbed by the blood, giving us an immediate shot of energy followed by a sudden fall in energy. Simple carbohydrates include sweets like candy, cookies and desserts and also anything made with white flour—including sandwiches made with white bread, white rice, flour tortillas, etc. You may notice that after a lunch of a sandwich on a French roll, an hour later you suddenly feel tired. That's because white flour has almost the same effect on the bloodstream as straight table sugar.

Complex carbohydrates, on the other hand, are made up of starches and fibers, and break down into glucose very slowly. In doing so, they can provide a consistent supply of energy for sustained periods of time, rather than suddenly and all at once.

Foods that are high in complex carbohydrates are also naturally low in fat, making you feel satisfied when you eat them, and are loaded with fiber, which is good for our digestive systems. (We'll talk about fiber a little later in this chapter.) In their unprocessed form, foods that contain complex carbohydrates are usually also loaded with essential vitamins and minerals. Foods high in complex carbohydrates include:

▶Vegetables—in salads and soups as well as raw and cooked vegetables and potatoes
▶Whole grains—bread, pasta, cereals made from whole grains (not processed), brown rice
▶Legumes—fresh and dried beans, peas and lentils
▶Seeds and nuts (eat in moderation as these are high in fat)

Protein

We need protein to build and repair tissues. The amino acids that make up proteins are used by the body in the production of enzymes, hormones and the antibodies that fight disease.

There is a lot of debate over whether or not people who work out regularly have greater protein needs than people who do not. Some say that since exercisers are building and repairing muscle tissue more often than non-

> *Carbohydrates are converted by the body into glucose, which fuels the brain, the nervous system and the muscles.*

exercisers, they need more protein. Part of the issue is what is meant by "more." More than the average American diet? Well, making a comparison to the average American diet is probably not a good idea, since the average American diet is loaded with protein and fat.

That's because despite our increased knowledge of nutrition, one out of five people is still eating a greasy cheeseburger for lunch. Certainly it has protein, and plenty of it, but it also comes with an artery-clogging quantity of fat. That same person is probably having red meat at one or two more meals of the day—maybe bacon and eggs for breakfast or a big steak for dinner. That "average" diet is way too high in fat, and it is probably unnecessarily high in protein as well. While eating too much protein is not going to harm you the way eating too much fat is, it is still tough on the body.

On the other hand, many people who exercise a lot or who are trying to lose weight turn to a high-carbohydrate diet. This is a great idea for everyone—but sometimes in our quest to eat all those good complex carbs we forget to get an equally good dose of protein.

In examining many athletes' and exercisers' diets, nutritionists have found that often these diets only provide about 20 to 30 grams of protein a day, which falls short of the recommended daily allowance of about 40-60 grams per day. That is going to the other extreme of the average American diet. While the athlete's high-carbohy-

> *The most important concept to keep in mind about protein is quality.*

drate diet is a better extreme, it still will not provide optimal nutrition.

Quality in Protein Sources

I believe the most important concept to keep in mind about protein is quality. When most of us think of protein, we think of meat—beef, chicken, fish, pork, etc. Protein is attainable from meat, as everyone knows, but is equally attainable from plant sources. Ideally, the majority of your protein intake should be from non-animal sources. Too much meat is definitely unhealthy, for two reasons. First, it is very high in fat and cholesterol, and we all know the evils of those. And second, almost all beef, pork and poultry comes from animals raised in feed lots, where they are fed synthetic growth hormones, antibiotics and other chemicals and also are subject to pesticide residues. All of that goes into the meat you cook and eat.

If you do eat meat, be sure it is as lean and clean as possible. Stick to chicken and fish as often as possible, and remove the skin. If you love beef and pork and can't live without them, save them for special occasions and stick to the leanest cuts. Also, watch your portion sizes. You can eat meat without making it the main portion of the meal. Above all, give up or greatly reduce the amount of processed, cured and smoked meats you eat—these are repositories of carcinogenic chemicals in addition to being high in fat.

You may have heard that animal protein is better for you than non-animal protein because our bodies can use it more efficiently. This is a myth that needs to be dispelled. It is true that animal proteins are complete proteins—they contain all of the essential amino acids that our bodies need, but can't manufacture. Non-animal proteins available in rice, beans, seeds and nuts do not contain all of the essential amino acids, *unless they are properly combined with other foods*. This is the only consideration when getting protein from non-animal sources—they must be combined properly.

It's easy: just combine grains (rice, cereals, breads, etc.) with legumes (fresh or dried beans, peas, lentils) and all the amino acids our bodies need will be represented. Or you can combine dairy products (milk, yogurt, cheese, etc.) with grains, or nuts and seeds with legumes.

Combining Foods to Make Proteins

If you think all this food combining is too cumbersome when you are hungry, just think of how many non-meat complete proteins are a part of the diet you already eat:
▶low-fat cheese sandwich on whole wheat bread
▶low-fat milk and cereal
▶beans and rice (burritos)
▶low-fat yogurt and granola
▶lentil soup or pea soup with a whole wheat roll

Each of these combinations can provide between 15 and 40 grams of protein, depending on the size of your portion.

How Much is Enough?

In terms of protein amounts, I would say that the best thing you can do is see what feels right for you, and then choose as much non-animal protein as possible. Adults need 40-60 grams of protein a day, and regular exercisers may find that they feel stronger with an additional 20 grams or so per day. Just be sure that if you are getting this much protein, you are getting it from low-fat sources. Gone are the days when athletes were served meat as their pre-competition meal; now sports nutritionists insist on complex carbohydrates like pasta and brown rice.

It's relatively simple to get enough low-fat protein in your diet. Consider eating some of the following good-for-you foods:

▶half a chicken breast (skinned, baked or broiled)—20 grams protein
▶tuna, 4 oz. (water-packed)—30 grams protein
▶rice and beans, 1 cup each—20 grams protein
▶cottage cheese, 1 cup (low-fat)—30 grams protein
▶non-fat or low-fat milk, 1 cup—10 grams protein

It's best if you spread out your protein intake throughout the day. The body is best suited to processing only about 20-30 grams of protein at a time.

Fat

Just hearing the word "fat" probably makes you shudder, as fat certainly has gotten a lot of bad press lately. We've all heard the warnings by now. Excess fat in our diets is blamed for arteriosclerosis, chronic heart disease, cancer, etc. But don't forget that fat is also an important nutrient source for the body—it keeps you warm, lubricates your cells, and helps to absorb important vitamins and minerals into your body.

Fat comes in saturated forms, such as butter and lard, and unsaturated forms, such as plant oils. The saturated fats are the ones to watch especially carefully, as they contain large amounts of

> *Don't forget that fat is also an important nutrient source for the body.*

cholesterol. Unsaturated fats have just as many calories as other fats, but they do not contain cholesterol and they do provide us with an essential fatty acid—linoleic acid.

Understanding Unsaturated Fats

Generally you are better off sticking to unsaturated plant fats, such as canola, safflower and corn oil, but beware of the so-called "tropical oils"—coconut and palm oil. These are actually highly saturated fats, and are commonly found in processed foods. Also beware of margarines, which at one time were touted as the perfect healthy swap for butter. Margarine, although made of unsaturated fats, is put through a hydrogenation process that makes it as harmful and almost as saturated as the saturated fats themselves. (Coconut and palm oils are almost always hydrogenated as well.) Also remember that regular margarine has just as many calories as butter, unless it is one of the new "light" margarines. These light margarines are lower in calories than butter, but still I would not recommend using them very often. They are largely a conglomeration of chemicals and hydrogenated oils.

All calories are not equal— some are more fattening than others.

A few words on storing vegetable oils: Always refrigerate them after opening to protect them from the process of oxidation, which makes oil go rancid and causes undesirable chemical changes. Olive oil is the only vegetable oil that can last long without refrigeration.

All Calories are Not Equal

You've probably heard that all calories are not equal—that calories from fat are actually more fattening than calories from other sources. It's true—carbohydrates and proteins both weigh in at only 4 calories per gram, while fats weigh in at a whopping 9 to 11 calories per gram! That means you're getting two and a half times more calories from fat than from equal amounts of carbohydrates or protein. As you can see, it is a lot smarter to get your calories from carbohydrates. Not only can you eat more with less calories to worry about, but the calories you get from carbohydrates are a lot more efficient and easily used by the body.

Also, keep in mind that the body converts dietary fat into body fat with much greater ease than it does with carbohydrates and proteins. The body burns calories in the process of digestion, but some foods are easier to digest than others and require fewer calories. The foods that are easiest to digest are fats, so fewer calories are burned in the process of digesting them. The human body requires only about three percent of fat's calories to digest fats, while it takes 20 percent of carbohydrate's calories to digest carbohydrates. So the other 97 percent of fat's calories are left for energy use, or they are stored as fat. Carbohydrates only have 80 percent of their calories left after digestion, to be used as energy or stored as fat.

This is a very significant point to understand about fats. Back when counting calories was all the rage, people used to think that all they had to do was eat whatever they wanted, but stop eating when they hit their calorie limit for the day. So eating 1400 calories of ice cream was considered the same as eating 1400 calories of carrots. But now we understand that that is NOT the case. Actually, according to the digestion rate above, eating 1400 fat calories will provide the body with 1358 calories for energy use and fat storage. But eating 1400 carbohydrate or protein calories will provide the body with only 1120 calories for energy use and fat storage. So you actually give your body 238 more calories by eating fat calories.

Less Fat = Less Fat

Less fat in your diet means less fat on your body, pure and simple. Where is fat found? Well, it is a natural part of many animal foods, such as meat and cheese. It is used as a cooking agent in fried foods, and it is often added in food preparation in sauces and the like. A tremendous amount of fat is "hidden" in processed foods.

Should we simply avoid all fat? No, because we do need it in our diet, but we need it only in very small amounts. The body's daily requirement for essential fatty acids can be met with one tablespoon of polyunsaturated fat. I recommend that no more than 20 percent of your total daily calories come from fat. That means that if you eat a diet of about 2000 calories of food a day, you should not have more than 400 calories of fat, or about 40 grams of fat a day.

The American Heart Association recommends that the fat level in your diet should be less than 30 percent, but they definitely agree that even lower is better. Their level is set at 30 percent because even that is a radical and difficult change for many people—the average American diet is over forty percent fat! Some diets, like the well-known Pritikin diet or the new Dean Ornish diet, keep fats as low as 10% of total daily calories. This requires very restrictive eating, but it is also very healthy eating.

Cholesterol

Cholesterol is the waxy substance in body tissues that is associated with hardening of the arteries and heart disease. Cholesterol is also an essential substance in our systems, though, one which we need to survive. It forms cell membranes, lines our nerves, and makes up much of our brain tissue. But too much cholesterol is not good, and more specifically, too much of the wrong kind of cholesterol is not good. You see, the body has two different types of cholesterol—HDL (high-density lipoprotein or "good cholesterol") and LDL (low-density lipoprotein or "bad cholesterol.") It is the balance between these two types of cholesterol that is so critical to good health.

HDLs actually remove potentially damaging cholesterol from the arteries and transport it to the liver for waste removal. LDLs are the cholesterol that line the walls of the arteries, narrowing them and making it harder for blood to circulate.

Cholesterol is present in many of the foods we eat, particularly animal fats such as milk products, eggs and meat. Our goal should be to keep our total blood cholesterol level below 180-200 milligrams, while keeping our LDLs low and our HDLs high. But even a total blood cholesterol number higher than 200 milligrams can be okay, as long as the balance between LDLs and HDLs is satisfactory. A higher level of HDLs can support a higher overall level of cholesterol. If you get your cholesterol tested, always ask for a breakdown of the the LDLs and HDLs in your total cholesterol amount.

If you have trouble with cholesterol, you should raise your HDLs by

Less fat in your diet means less fat on your body, pure and simple.

doing exercise such as aerobics and weight training, and you should lower your LDLs by eliminating or greatly reducing high-cholesterol foods. Scientists are not certain why regular exercise has a positive effect on HDL levels, but studies have shown that it seems to help establish a good mix of cholesterol in the blood.

Here are some of the foods that are among the worst offenders in terms of cholesterol: egg yolks, veal, lamb, beef, pork, liver and other organ meats, butter, cheeses, and the skin of poultry. They should all be on the "wanted for attempted murder" list.

Water

Above all others, one substance is extremely vital to the body. We need it almost as much as we need oxygen, and we need it more than we need food, and yet it is the nutrient we most neglect. It is inexpensive and is found virtually everywhere. It's water, of course, and we've all heard that we should be drinking six to eight glasses a day. People who exercise a lot should drink even more.

Our bodies have very good defense mechanisms. But when it comes to fluids, our bodies' defenses are lacking. They don't always remind us to drink when we need to—we can need water before we actually experience feeling thirsty. Many people "forget" to drink enough water and practically live in a semi-dehydrated state.

Water is vital to the body. Don't let your body beg you for a drink.

Once again, the name of the game is awareness.

If you do nothing else, increase your water consumption consciously to eight glasses per day. Do it slowly over a period of several weeks. Add a glass of water per day and get to the point where your base is eight glasses per day. You will not believe the positive changes in your energy level and appearance.

If you find yourself running to the bathroom very often after making this change, don't worry. After a few days of "increased activity" in the bathroom, things will subside back to normal. As with all the changes I've mentioned here, the body needs a few days to get adjusted.

One note about water consumption: The quality of tap water varies greatly throughout the world, even throughout the United States. Rarely will you find tap water that has not been tainted by chemicals, either in the chlorination process or through ground seepage. In general, I recommend buying bottled water or installing a water filter in your kitchen. The small cost is definitely worth the investment in your long-term health.

There are other ways to provide your body with water besides drinking it from the tap. Fruits and vegetables are loaded with water, which is why they taste so good when you are thirsty. Almost all fruits are ninety percent water. Make sure you eat plenty of these in addition to drinking your eight glasses of water a day.

What to Eat

If someone asked me to tell them what the ten most important rules are for good nutrition and an enjoyable diet, I'd tell them these:

▶Substitute low-fat for high-fat foods (non-fat frozen yogurt for ice cream, etc.)
▶ Eat food as close to its natural state as possible. Minimize consumption of processsed foods.
▶Cut down on red meat consumption.

▶Make complex carbohydrates 60-75% of your daily diet for energy and fiber.

▶Avoid salt and salty foods.

▶Drink lots of water.

▶Reduce your consumption of alcohol and caffeine.

▶Reduce your reliance on sweets and sugary foods.

▶Avoid food additives.

▶Seek balance and moderation in your diet.

The first rule is perhaps the most significant one in that it expresses a philosophy of substitution that can teach you to really enjoy a better way of eating. When most people think of changing their diet, they think of depriving themselves of food they like. But wouldn't it be easier if we could just substitute some foods for other foods, never allowing ourselves to go hungry or be without the kinds of food we want? In fact, this rule, "substitute low-fat foods for high-fat foods," may be the easiest and most painless way to trim fat from our diets.

The substitution attitude is useful to develop. Instead of viewing your changing eating habits as some kind of deprivation, you can learn to eat foods that you enjoy that are also good for you. There is no deprivation involved. I know people who have gone from eating red meat three or four times a week for dinner to just having an occasional lean steak once a month. By eating chicken and fish regularly instead of red meat, they don't even notice the difference. You'll find that by gradually cutting down on your intake of unhealthy foods and substituting healthy ones, the unhealthy foods will become less appealing.

Fiber

Your body is not supposed to absorb all the food you eat. In fact, you want to increase the amount of food you eat that the body cannot absorb—whole grain and unrefined products which are high in FIBER. The fiber found in unprocessed foods can actually help reduce the risk of colon cancer, diverticulosis, diabetes and heart disease. Fiber is found only in plant foods, and is easily obtained by eating whole grain breads, brown rice, bulgur wheat, oatmeal, bran cereals, bran muffins, and bran flakes. It is better to eat whole foods to get your fiber than to add bran to everything, as too much bran can actually rob your body of some minerals.

Fiber leaves a residue in the intestines, since the human body cannot absorb it. This residue is actually good for the digestive tract, and it also aids in controlling cholesterol levels. The effect of fiber that is immediately noticeable is that it fills you up— but with few calories.

High fiber foods include all of the foods mentioned previously plus vegetables and fruits. You can also get plenty of fiber in your diet by eating cereals such as shredded wheat and puffed wheat, or making whole grain pancakes, waffles and muffins. Other good sources include whole wheat bagels, popcorn, beans, whole wheat noodles, rye crackers, and corn tortillas.

Try to replace any low-fiber foods you eat with high-fiber foods. Watch

> *Try to replace any low-fiber foods you eat with high-fiber foods.*

out for the foods on the following list—if you're eating any of them, try to replace them with high-fiber choices. The foods in parentheses are good high-fiber substitutions.

Low Fiber Foods (and good substitutions)

▶ white bread and white flour products **(whole grain bread and whole grain products)**

▶ cream of wheat **(cooked oatmeal or low fat whole-grain granola)**

▶ corn flakes **(whole grain cereals such as shredded wheat and bran)**

▶ flour tortillas **(corn tortillas)**

▶ crackers and cookies **(whole grain crackers such as Ry-Krisps)**

▶ corn and potato chips **(popcorn or baked tortilla chips)**

▶ bagels made with white flour **(whole wheat bagels)**

▶ muffins made with white flour **(whole grain muffins)**

▶ Bisquick pancakes or waffles **(buckwheat or whole grain pancakes or waffles)**

▶ white rice **(brown rice)**

▶ white flour pasta and noodles **(whole wheat pasta)**

▶ fruit juices **(whole fruits)**

▶ vegetable juices **(whole vegetables)**

Food Culprits

With all the emphasis on cutting the fat and adding fiber to our diets, we can't forget the other big dietary villains: sugar, salt, caffeine and food additives.

Sugar

Sugar, while supposedly harmless except for the possibility of tooth decay and its effects on our blood sugar levels, is responsible for a lot of empty calories—calories that could be spent on nutritive foods that would fuel our bodies and make us feel better. Our bodies have absolutely no need for sugar, and our eating it only stimulates the appetite to crave more. While complex carbohydrates give us the glycogen we need for long-term, sustained energy, sugar gives us only a temporary high—which is followed by a plummet into fatigue and lethargy.

Many people say that they don't eat sweets. Although they may avoid the obvious sources of sugar, such as soft drinks, cookies, candy, and desserts, they may not realize how much sugar they are getting from other sources. Sugar is the number one additive in processed foods. It is used in bread, crackers, ketchup, cereals, spaghetti sauce, bouillon cubes, non-dairy creamers, cured meats—you name it. And it goes by many "hidden" names—fructose, dextrose, honey, maple or corn syrup, molasses....Watch for them on ingredient lists.

Salt

Salt, like sugar, is an acquired taste. Salt, or sodium, is needed by the body, but in very small amounts—amounts that occur naturally in the non-processed foods we eat. Too much sodium in the body can result in high blood pressure, which unfortunately often goes unnoticed until it causes a stroke or heart attack.

It would be virtually impossible not to get enough sodium in our diets, unless we were starving ourselves. Sodium is found in nearly everything we eat, and is found in excess in processed and canned foods. Some of the worst culprits are:

►canned soups
►frozen dinners
►fast foods
►cheeses
►smoked and processed meats
►snacks like potato chips, salted nuts, crackers
►condiments like ketchup and soy sauce
►pickles
►olives
►some breakfast cereals—read the labels
►instant hot cereals
►canned tomato and vegetable juices

There are no set recommendations for the amount of sodium in our diets, but a safe range is between 1500 and 2500 milligrams a day. The body actually needs only 220 milligrams a day. People who are on sodium-restricted diets are usually allowed less than one gram of sodium a day (1000 milligrams). If you stay right around two grams of sodium per day (2000 milligrams), you will be in a healthy range.

While you're leaning away from salt, you might want to lean toward potassium. Potassium has been found to prevent high blood pressure, and many people believe that a proper sodium-potassium balance in the body is critical to good health. Foods high in potassium include cantaloupe, bananas, potatoes, oranges, grapefruit, tomatoes, yellow squash, spinach, papaya and beans.

Caffeine

Caffeine is a habit that many people develop as young adults, and it often gets out of control. Caffeine is not recommended for a healthy diet because it overstimulates the nervous system, can increase your susceptibility to coronary artery disease and can eventually cause stomach ulcers. It is also a diuretic and so it depletes us of vitamins and minerals. It has been linked to an increase in appetite, craving for sweets, insomnia and nervousness. Caffeine is common-

ly associated with coffee and tea, but it is also found in soft drinks, chocolate, and many over-the-counter cold and headache remedies.

Food Additives

It is difficult for most people to eat a diet of only whole foods. For the sake of convenience, sometimes we just have to buy processed foods. When we do, there is more to watch out for than just fat, salt and sugar. We should also watch for the amounts of various food additives, which have been connected with risk factors for cancer. Generally, if you read the ingredient list on the package and it's very long and filled with all kinds of unknown words, you should probably eat something else. Of course, some food additives are safe, but in general you want to avoid anything with the following ingredients, which have been linked in some studies to cancer in laboratory animals.

►BHA or butylated hydroxyanisole
►BHT or butylated hydroxytoluene
►BVA or brominated vegetable oil
►propyl gallate
►saccharine
►sodium nitrate and sodium nitrite
►sulphur dioxide and sodium bisulphate
►quinine
►artificial colorings such as Citrus Red No. 2, Red No. 3, Yellow No. 5, Blue No. 1 and 2

Moderation

I don't suggest that we should spend the rest of our lives on a salt-free, sugar-free, caffeine-free, additive-free diet. I do not recommend that anyone completely deprive themselves of anything, unless forced to do so for medical reasons. But we could reduce our intake of the foods that our bodies don't need and by doing so increase our intake of the foods our bodies do need. Reducing our reliance on salt, fat, sugar and the other "food culprits" can be done gradually. You won't miss them as much if you cut back slowly. The main idea is to develop sensible eating habits that you will follow most of the time.

Become aware of the foods that are good for you and focus on them. Personally, my diet has improved a lot over the years. For example, when I was growing up, I liked to butter my bread like everyone else I knew. Of course, I didn't have any awareness that butter is loaded with fat and not good for me, and truly I didn't care anyway. Now that I'm older and a little more aware of the importance of what goes in my body, I try to avoid using butter. Now if I taste a slice of toast with butter on it, it tastes very strange to me.

The same is true with coffee. Even when I was competing in track, I used to have several cups of coffee per day. In fact I'd have a cup of coffee or two before I started my training each day. But I used to feel noticeable changes in my energy level—it was never very consistent. I was drinking two to three cups of coffee per meal, which added up to eight or nine cups per day!

Over a period of time I started to adjust my coffee intake. I took time to go from one change to the next, and by doing so I didn't feel any "withdrawals" or deprivation. I was able to develop control over this habit.

Tips for Avoiding the Food Culprits

▶Avoid processed foods as much as possible. These are great sources of both sugar and salt, because these two ingredients add "flavor" to food that has been stripped of it. Read the labels on the processed foods you do buy. The list of ingredients is always in order of proportionate amounts—the first ingredient is the main ingredient, the last ingredient is a negligible amount. If sugar or salt is listed among the first several

ingredients, choose another product. Remember that sugar comes under many names.

▶When cooking or baking at home, reduce the amount of sugar in recipes by half. The finished product will still be delicious, and most people will not be able to tell the difference.

▶If you are craving something sweet, try a piece of fresh fruit and see if that curbs your appetite. Fruit is just like dessert, but with all those extra vitamins and minerals along for the ride.

▶Do not add salt while cooking. If you must add salt, the only time to do it is when the food is on your plate, after you have tasted it and are certain that it needs salt. Never salt your food without tasting it first. Try using one of the "lite" salt brands, which are half sodium and half potassium chloride.

▶Learn to substitute herbal teas or decaffeinated teas and coffee for caffeinated ones. If you drink decaffeinated teas or coffee, make sure that they are decaffeinated by "water process." That is the safest and purest method of decaffeination.

▶If you have to have a "drink," have it only in small amounts. Don't drink alcoholic drinks when you are thirsty. Quench your thirst with water first; then have a drink if you still want it.

▶Always have healthy foods on hand so that you don't have to resort to fast foods or processed foods when you are in a hurry and hungry. Fresh fruit and low-fat whole grain crackers are the perfect snack foods that you can always have on hand.

▶Keep in mind that your food is the fuel your body runs on. When you want to eat something, think to yourself, "What food will give me lots of energy and make me feel good if I eat it?"

The more you ask that question, rather than just grabbing the first edible thing you see, the better you will eat.

Cooking

Several cooking techniques can improve the nutritive content of your food.
►Trim all visible fat from meats.
►Season vegetables with spices, lemon, wine, garlic, onions and mushrooms.
►Take the skin off of poultry and fish.
►Use buttermilk, cottage cheese and yogurt as a base for sauces and salad dressings, instead of sour cream.
►Use half the sugar that is called for in recipes.
►Use nonstick pots, pans and baking dishes, so less oil is needed to keep foods from sticking.
►Learn new recipes for boiling, poaching, baking, barbecuing, microwaving and steaming foods. Avoid frying, especially deep-frying.

Tips for Restaurant Eating

It's not that difficult to maintain a healthy diet, even if you eat out often. But again, awareness is the key. I find that most restaurants will prepare food to my requests. If I ask for a broiled, skinless breast of chicken, intead of sauteed, it can be done. If I ask for a baked potato, served dry, it can be made. Both are actually easier and simpler to prepare. Many think that when they eat out or are invited to dinner by a friend, it's time to splurge. Think of it this way—your friend may be picking up the tab, but you are going to pay the price!

When eating out, keep these tips in mind:

►Order a salad with lots of fresh vegetables, but be careful about salad dressings. Ask if they have a low-fat dressing; if not, ask for oil and vinegar that you can mix yourself or for a few lemon slices. If you must have regular salad dressing, ask for it on the side, and then only use a small amount. Leave the rest.

►Soups are usually a good choice in restaurants, provided they are not cream-based. Ask. If the waiter or waitress assures you there is no cream or whole-fat milk in the soup, order it.

►If you order any dishes that come with sauces, get the sauce on the side, or ask your waiter to leave it off altogether. If the sauce is on the side, you get to decide how much of it you will eat.

►Order your food baked or broiled.

►Try to avoid cheese or cheese-covered menu items, or ask that the chef use less cheese on your order or serve it on the side.

►At breakfast, order whole wheat or whole grain toast and ask for it to be served dry, or without butter. At other meals, have the waiter remove the pats of butter from the table, or keep just one and try not to finish it.

►Avoid alcohol. If everyone else is drinking, you can order a sparkling water, half mineral water and half fruit juice, a light beer, or a Virgin Mary.

Good For You Foods
(A Good Basic Shopping List)

►nonfat and low-fat milk, yogurt and other dairy products

►buttermilk

►fish and shellfish

►chicken—white meat only with no skin

►turkey—white meat only with no skin

►beans—dried or cooked without fat

►brown rice

►corn tortillas

►all fresh vegetables and fruits (limit consumption of avocados, coconut and olives as these are high in fat)

►whole grain breads and crackers without added fat

►tofu

►plain popcorn

►cereals without added fat and sugar

Not Good For You Foods
(Your UN-Shopping List)

►whole milk and full-fat dairy products (sour cream, cream cheese, ice cream)

►gravies

►non-dairy creamers and products

►full-fat cheeses

►beef, lamb, pork

►all processed meats—ham, bacon, sausage, salami, luncheon meats

►canned foods

►sweetened cereals

►cream-based soups and sauces

►fried foods

►processed foods

►white flour bread products

►crackers and cookies, snack chips, candy, doughnuts

►mayonnaise

►butter, margarine, saturated oils like coconut and palm oils

►full-fat salad dressings

►sweet drinks—sodas, sweet mineral waters, etc.

Warm-Up And Stretch

▶No matter what physical activity you are about to perform, it is always important to start with a general warm-up. A general warm-up should consist of a short, easy aerobics portion to raise your heart rate and get your blood circulating, followed by specific warm-up and stretching exercises. A general warm-up helps prevent injury and gives you a better overall workout. So, before you do any exercise, warm up!

Short, Easy Aerobics To Start

▶The first part of the warm-up consists of three to five minutes of light aerobic activity. This can be marching or jogging in place, fast walking, low impact knee lifts, side stepping or any easy aerobics. Then, move on to the specific warm-up and stretching exercises shown on the following pages.

WARM-UP AND STRETCHING EXERCISES

Shoulder Rolls

For the neck, shoulders and upper back.

▶Stand with your feet shoulder-width apart and your knees slightly bent. Relax your arms by your sides and look straight forward, keeping your back flat, your shoulders relaxed and your abdominal muscles pulled in.

Slowly roll your shoulders, lifting them forward and up and then back and down, forming a circle. Breathe in as you roll your shoulders forward and exhale as you release them to the back.

Perform this exercise eight times starting forward and eight times starting to the back. When starting to the back, breathe in as you lift your shoulders to the back and exhale as you roll them forward.

Chin Drops and Head Turns

For the neck and spine.

▶Start with the same body position as with Shoulder Rolls.

Slowly drop your chin to your chest and then lift your head back up to a neutral position, looking straight forward. Perform this exercise eight times, breathing normally.

Then turn your head to the right and to the left, looking side to side. Look to each side eight times, breathing normally.

Side Twists

For the lower back and abdominals.

▶Start with your feet shoulder width apart, knees slightly bent, back flat, abdominals pulled in and your buttocks tucked in.

Pull your elbows into your waist and slowly twist your body from the waist up, moving side-to-side and keeping your lower body stationary and firm. Keep your knees directly over your toes at all times.

Exhale on each twist and repeat this exercise eight times to each side.

Full Side Reaches

For the feet, calves, thighs, middle back, shoulders and arms.

▶Start with your feet shoulder width apart, knees slightly bent, back flat and abdominals pulled in.

Fully extend the legs while reaching overhead at an angle to the opposite side.

Breathe out on the extension and repeat eight times to each side.

Back Rolls

For the lower and middle back.

▶Start with your feet shoulder width apart and knees bent, leaning slightly forward from the hips. Your hands should rest on the center of your thighs, supporting your weight. Keep your back flat and abdominals pulled in.

Slowly pull your abdominals in and roll your back up while tucking your pelvis. Release to the starting position with a flat back.

Breathe in before starting this exercise, and then exhale as you roll your back and inhale as you release to the starting position. Repeat this exercise eight times.

Side Lunges

For the quadriceps, inner thighs and buttocks.

▶Start with your feet twice your shoulder width apart. Place your palms on the center of your thighs, keeping your back flat and your abdominals pulled in. Lean slightly forward, and slowly shift your weight to one side, dropping your opposite hip toward the floor. Do not bend your knee so far that it goes beyond the line of your toes. You will feel the stretch in your thigh.

Hold briefly and then slowly shift your weight to the other side. Exhale as you go to each side, breathing in as you pass through center. Repeat this exercise eight times to each side.

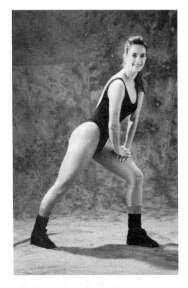

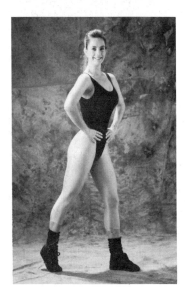

Calf Stretch and Heel Raises

For the feet, calves and hamstrings.

▶Start with your feet twice your shoulder width apart. Turn to one side so both feet are pointing in the same direction, one foot in front of the other. Keep both heels down and slightly bend your front knee so it is positioned over your heel.

Lean forward, placing both hands on your bent knee, keeping your back flat and your abdominals pulled in. You should feel a stretch in the calf muscles of your rear leg. Hold for eight seconds while breathing normally.

Then straighten your upper body, place your hands on your hips and slowly lift and lower your rear heel up and down off the floor, flexing the calf muscle. Lift and release eight times, breathing out on the lift.

Shift to the other side and repeat the entire sequence.

Standing Hamstring Stretch

For the hamstrings.

▶Start with your feet shoulder width apart. Turn to the side, so both feet are pointing in the same direction. Keeping your front leg straight, bend your rear knee and rock back on your front heel. Place your palms on the bent knee of your rear leg. Flex your front foot, lean slightly forward with a flat back and keep your abdominals pulled in.

Sit into the stretch, lowering your buttocks toward the floor. You should feel the stretch in the back of your front leg (hamstring). To increase the stretch, readjust your feet to a slightly wider position. Breathe normally while holding this stretch for eight seconds, then shift to the other side and repeat.

Bicep Curls

For the biceps (front of the upper arm).

▶Start with your feet shoulder width apart and knees slightly bent. Keep your back flat, abdominals pulled in and elbows tucked in at the sides of your waist.

Clench your fists and slowly raise your hands toward your shoulders, contracting your biceps muscles. Lower your arms to the starting position.

Exhale as you are squeezing your arms up and inhale as you release your arms down. Repeat eight times.

Triceps Extension

For the triceps (back of the upper arm).

▶Start with your feet apart, knees slightly bent and back flat. Lean your upper body slightly forward, keeping your abdominals pulled in. Your elbows should be bent, fists clenched and at waist level.

Slowly extend the arms back, contracting the triceps muscle until the elbows are straight, and then return to the starting position. Avoid locking your elbows on the extension.

Exhale on the extension and inhale on the release. Repeat this exercise eight times.

Triceps and Shoulder Stretch

For the triceps and posterior deltoids.

▶Start with your feet apart, knees slightly bent and back straight. Keep your abdominals pulled in. Bring your right arm in front of your right shoulder with your elbow bent, holding it stationary with your left hand.

Using the palm of your left hand, press your right arm to the back, stretching your triceps and shoulder. Hold for eight seconds while breathing normally, then repeat on the other side.

Shoulder Stretch

For the shoulders.

▶Start with your feet apart and
your knees slightly bent. Keep
your back flat and your abdominals pulled in. Bring one arm
across your chest, with a slight
bend in the elbow. Support it with
your opposite hand.

Pull your extended arm farther
across your body with the palm of
your opposite hand. Hold for eight
seconds while breathing normally
and then repeat on the other side.

Low Impact / High Impact Aerobics

LOW IMPACT AEROBICS

During the low impact aerobics segment, you should always keep one foot in contact with the floor. You should be able to breathe comfortably during the whole workout.

To increase your cardiovascular work, increase the size and range of your movement or the extension of your arms. If you find yourself working too hard (if you feel very out of breath and uncomfortable), reduce the size of your movements or eliminate your arm movements altogether.

The low impact aerobics sequence is to be performed three to four times in succession. For a more advanced workout, do this routine twice and immediately go to the high impact aerobics routine that follows and perform it twice.

HIGH IMPACT AEROBICS

The high impact workout is designed to provide a high level of cardiovascular work and should be performed only after you feel comfortable doing the low impact workout. You should be able to breathe comfortably during the whole workout.

To increase your cardiovascular work, increase the size and range of your movement or the extension of your arms. If you find yourself working too hard, reduce the size of your movements or just march in place. Repeat this routine three to four times in succession or do it twice following two repetitions of the low impact workout.

LOW IMPACT AEROBICS

►March in place with high knee lifts.

Perform eight repetitions on each side.

▶Step side to side with your arms low.

Perform eight repetitions on each side.

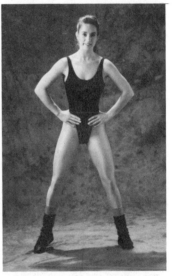

▶Step side to side and extend your arms overhead.

Perform eight repetitions on each side.

▶Lift alternating knees, bringing your elbow to your opposite knee.

Perform eight repetitions on each side.

▶Lift your knees, bringing your elbow to your opposite knee and adding arm circles overhead.

Perform eight repetitions on each side.

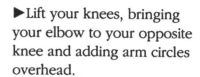

▶Step side to side with a hamstring curl (bring your heel to your buttocks).

Perform eight repetitions on each side.

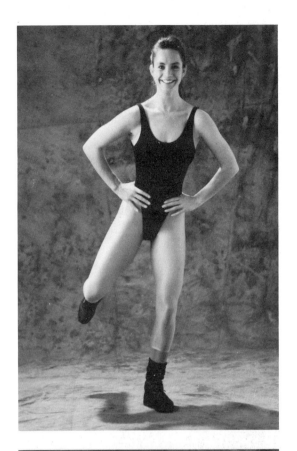

►Lunge to the side with your hands on your waist.

Perform eight repetitions on each side.

►Then march in place with high knees for eight repetitions on each side.

►Lunge to the side with your arms high.

Perform eight repetitions on each side.

►Lunge to the rear with your arms high.

Perform eight repetitions on each side.

►Then march in place with high knees for eight repetitions on each side.

▶Take a rock step forward and back with one leg four times. The other leg stays at the center, stepping up and down. Then change sides (right, left, right, left).

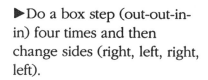

▶Do a box step (out-out-in-in) four times and then change sides (right, left, right, left).

►March for three counts, kick forward for one count and then change sides (right, left, right, left).

►Then march in place with high knees for eight repetitions on each side.

►Go back to page 76 and repeat the low impact workout three to four times, or do it twice and move on to the high impact workout that follows.

HIGH IMPACT AEROBICS

Start with a low-impact warm up:

▶March in place with high knees (16 repetitions on each side).

▶Lunge to the side with high arms (16 repetitions on each side).

Now begin the high impact cardiovascular work:

▶March in place with high knees (eight repetitions on each side).

►Jump rope (eight repetitions on each side).

►Then march in place with high knees (eight repetitions on each side).

Alternate this sequence three times.

▶Jog in place (eight repetitions on each side).

▶Then march in place with high knees (eight repetitions on each side).

Repeat this sequence twice.

▶Low kick to the front with a hop (eight repetitions on each side).

▶Then march in place with high knees (eight repetitions on each side).

Repeat this sequence twice.

▶Single knee lifts with a hop, pushing your arms overhead (eight repetitions on each side).

▶March in place with high knees (eight repetitions on each side).

Repeat this sequence twice.

▶Jumping jacks (eight repetitions).

▶March in place with high knees (eight repetitions on each side).

Repeat this sequence twice.

▶Run in place (double-time) for 16 repetitions on each side.

▶March in place with high knees for eight repetitions on each side.

Repeat this sequence twice, then go back to the beginning of the high impact workout and do the whole routine three to four times. Or just do it twice if you combine it with two repetitions of the low impact workout.

Aerobic Cool-Down and General Cool-Down

The cool-down routine is designed to allow your heart rate to gradually decrease after aerobic exercise. This routine is important for the health of your heart and will also actively stretch some the muscles used during exercise.

Following an aerobic workout, whether it's walking, running, or high or low impact aerobics, it is necessary to continue working aerobically at a significantly reduced level to allow your heart rate to come down slowly. This is what is known as the Aerobic Cool-down. It should be followed by the General Cool-down, which stretches the major muscle groups.

AEROBIC COOL-DOWN

▶March in place with high knees—16 times each leg

▶Alternate low impact heel touches to the front—16 times each leg

▶Alternate toe and heel touches to the back—16 times each leg

▶Side steps—16 times each leg

Repeat the entire sequence twice.

►Stand with your feet apart and knees slightly bent. Take three deep breaths, circling your arms overhead as you inhale and releasing your arms to your sides as you exhale.

GENERAL COOL-DOWN

Full Side Reaches

▶Start with your feet shoulder width apart, knees slightly bent, back flat and abdominals pulled in. Fully extend the legs while reaching overhead at a slight angle to the opposite side.

Breathe out on the extension.

Repeat eight times to each side.

Back Rolls

▶Start with your feet shoulder width apart, knees bent, leaning slightly forward from the hips. Your hands should rest on the center of your thighs, supporting your weight. Keep your back flat and abdominals pulled in.

Tighten your abdominals further and roll your back up while tucking your pelvis, then release to the starting position with a flat back.

Breathe in before starting this exercise, and then exhale as you roll your back and inhale as you release to the starting position.

Repeat this exercise eight times.

Side Lunges

▶Start with your feet twice your shoulder width apart. Place your palms on the center of your thighs, keeping your back flat and your abdominals pulled in. Slowly shift your weight to your left side, dropping your right hip toward the floor and rising up on your right heel. Do not bend your left knee so far that it goes beyond the line of your toes.

Hold briefly and then slowly shift your weight to the other side. Exhale as you go to each side, breathing in as you pass through center.

Repeat this exercise eight times to each side.

BODIES IN MOTION

Calf and Shoulder Stretch

▶Start with your feet twice your shoulder width apart. Turn to one side so that both feet are pointing in the same direction, one foot in front of the other. Keep both heels down and slightly bend the front knee so that it is positioned over the heel.

Lean forward, lengthening both arms overhead to stretch your shoulders. Keep your back flat and your abdominals pulled in. You should feel a stretch in the calf muscles of your rear leg as well as in your upper body and shoulders.

Shift to the other side and repeat.

Standing Hamstring Stretch

▶Start with your feet shoulder width apart. Turn to the side, so both feet are pointing in the same direction. Keeping your front leg straight, bend your rear knee and rock back on your front heel. Place your palms on the bent knee of your rear leg for support.

Flex your front foot, lean slightly forward with a flat back and keep your abdominals pulled in. Sit into the stretch, lowering your buttocks toward the floor. You should feel the stretch in the back of your front leg (hamstring).

To increase the stretch, readjust your feet to a slightly wider position. Breathe normally while holding this stretch, then shift to the other side and repeat.

Chest and Shoulder Stretch

▶Start with your feet apart, knees slightly bent and back straight. Keep your abdominals pulled in. Clasp your hands behind your back and pull down, stretching your chest and shoulders. Avoid arching your back.

Switch hands and repeat.

Triceps and Shoulder Stretch

▶Start with your feet apart, knees slightly bent and back straight. Keep your abdominals pulled in. Bring your arm to the side of your head with your elbow bent.

Using the palm of your opposite hand, press your arm to the back, stretching the triceps and shoulder.

Repeat on the other side.

Shoulder Rolls

▶Stand with your feet shoulder-
width apart and your knees slightly
bent. Relax your arms by your
sides and look straight forward,
keeping your back flat, your shoulders relaxed and your abdominal
muscles pulled in. Slowly roll your
shoulders, lifting them forward and
up and then back and down, forming a circle.

Breathe in as you roll your shoulders forward and exhale as you
release them to the back.

Perform this exercise eight times
starting forward and eight times
starting to the back. When starting
to the back, breathe in as you lift
your shoulders to the back and
exhale as you roll them forward.

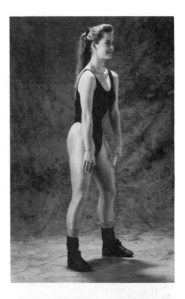

Deep Breaths

▶Start with your feet apart, knees slightly bent and back straight. Slowly circle your arms up overhead while breathing in, and release your arms as you exhale.

Repeat three times.

Progressive Flexibility Workout

▶The following routine is designed to increase your flexibility. It should be performed two to three times per week, directly after your cool-down, while your muscles are still warm. It can also be done on days that you don't exercise, but be sure to warm-up your body thoroughly first.

The most important part of flexibility training is stretching each muscle within the limits of comfort. Forcing a stretch, or over-stretching a muscle beyond what it can comfortably do, actually causes the muscle to contract in order to protect itself from being torn. This is the reverse of what you want to achieve—you want the muscle to lengthen, expand and relax in a stretch.

Pay attention to your breathing as you stretch. Don't hold your breath while stretching. If you exhale and inhale rhythmically, trying to relax into the stretch, you will stretch deeper and further.

I suggest that you do three sets of any given stretch. In the first set, you get into position, making sure you are maintaining good posture, and try to feel your range of movement by slowly breathing out. Then relax and let go of the stretch.

In the second set, start by taking a couple of deep breaths, and then on the third breath, slowly exhale and get back into position, trying to go a little further this time without feeling tense and uncomfortable. Keep breathing and reaching into the stretch. As you exhale, try to let all the tension in your body dissolve. Let go of the stretch and gently "shake out" the area being stretched.

In the third set, repeat what you did on set two, and try to go just a bit further, still maintaining a relaxed posture throughout the whole stretch. Remember, you are stretching to the point of your own limitation and not to the point of pain.

PROGRESSIVE FLEXIBILITY WORKOUT

Knee Tuck to Chest

▶Lie flat on your back, with one knee bent and your foot flat on the floor. Hold your other knee to your chest while grasping your hamstring behind your knee.

Open your knee until your leg is in a straight line. Hold it from behind and pull your knee further toward your chest to increase the stretch.

Repeat using the other leg.

Perform 3 sets:
Warm-up Set—Hold the position for 8 to 12 seconds.

Working Set—Take two deep breaths before starting, then hold the position for 12 to 15 seconds while stretching a little further.

Challenge Set—Take two deep breaths before starting, then hold the position for 12 to 15 seconds while stretching still further.

Knee Drop to Side

▶Lie flat on your back with both feet flat on the floor, knees bent, and arms stretched out to the right side. Drop both knees to the left, keeping your knees together.

Then drop both knees to the right and stretch your arms over to the left.

Perform 3 sets:
Warm-up Set—Hold the position for 8 to 12 seconds.

Working Set—Take two deep breaths before starting, then hold the position for 12 to 15 seconds while stretching a little further.

Challenge Set—Take two deep breaths before starting, then hold the position for 12 to 15 seconds while stretching still further.

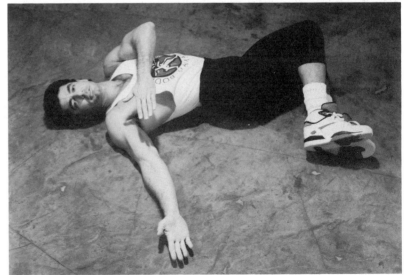

Quadriceps Stretch

▶Lying on your right side, hold your left ankle with your left hand and gently pull your leg to the rear, releasing your hip to feel the stretch in the thigh.

Change to the other side and repeat with the other leg.

Perform 3 sets:
Warm-up Set—Hold the position for 8 to 12 seconds.

Working Set—Take two deep breaths before starting, then hold the position for 12 to 15 seconds while stretching a little further.

Challenge Set—Take two deep breaths before starting, then hold the position for 12 to 15 seconds while stretching still further.

Lower Back/Hamstring Stretch

▶Begin in a seated position with your knees slightly bent. Sit up as tall as you can and pull your chest slightly toward your knees.

Straighten your legs partway. Reach for your ankles and pull your chest toward your knees while keeping your back flat.

Straighten your legs a little further. Reach for your ankles and pull your chest further toward your knees. Remember to keep your back flat.

Perform 3 sets:
Warm-up Set—Hold the position for 8 to 12 seconds.

Working Set—Take two deep breaths before starting, then hold the position for 12 to 15 seconds while stretching a little further.

Challenge Set—Take two deep breaths before starting, then hold the position for 12 to 15 seconds while stretching still further.

Straight Leg/ Bent Knee Stretch

▶Begin in a seated position, with one leg extended and your knee and toes pointing upward. The other leg is resting on the floor with the knee bent at a 45 degree angle. Place your hands behind your body for support and sit up straight.

Keeping the same body position, place your hands in front of you and lean slightly forward.

Turn your upper body toward your straight leg and lean slightly forward, reaching for your toes with your opposite hand. Repeat the entire sequence on the other side.

Perform three sets as described previously.

Straddle Stretch

▶Sit with your legs straddled apart, knees and feet pointing upward, hands placed behind your body for support. Sit up as straight as possible.

Place your hands in front of your body and lean slightly forward.

Increase your forward lean while keeping your back flat. Place your forearms on the floor, if possible.

Perform three sets as described previously.

Hips and Buttocks Stretch

▶Begin in a seated position, legs crossed in front of you, hands placed behind your body. Sit up as straight as possible.

Move your hands in front of your body, leaning forward while keeping your back flat.

Release your head and shoulders and relax your upper body forward.

Change your crossed legs and repeat.

Perform three sets as described previously.

Hugs

▶In a standing position with your feet shoulder width apart and your knees slightly bent, pull both arms across your chest with your elbows bent, placing your hands on opposite shoulders.

Switch the arm on top and repeat.

Perform three sets as described previously.

Chest and Shoulder Stretch

▶In a standing position, clasp your hands behind your back and pull downward, stretching your chest and shoulders. Avoid arching your back and keep your eyes forward.

Switch hands and repeat.

Perform three sets as described previously.

Triceps and Shoulder Stretch

▶In a standing position, bring your right arm to the side of your head with your elbow bent.

Using the palm of your left hand, press your right arm to the back, stretching the triceps and shoulder.

Switch arms and repeat on the other side.

Perform three sets as described previously.

Head Tilts

▶From a standing position, looking straight forward, slowly drop your right ear toward your right shoulder.

Repeat on your left side.

Perform three sets as described previously.

Chin Drop

▶From a standing position, look straight forward and place your hands behind your head.

Drop your chin to your chest, pulling gently with your hands to stretch your upper back and neck muscles.

Perform three sets as described previously.

Conditioning Workouts

These workouts are designed to improve your muscle strength and endurance. The exercises are not aerobic in nature; rather they are designed to tone and shape the major muscle groups of the body. If you have never lifted weights before, these are great routines to start training your muscles. If you currently lift weights, these workouts are excellent for the times in your life when you don't have access to your gym, club or normal exercise environment.

The following pages show two different routines (Conditioning Workouts #1 and #2). Perform each routine once per week to develop and maintain good muscular conditioning. For superior results, do each routine twice per week, so that you are doing one conditioning routine every other day.

In general, keep in mind the following guidelines while performing these exercises:

►Always keep your abdominals pulled in to help support your back (even when lying down).

►When standing, unless directed otherwise, keep your feet shoulder width apart, knees slightly bent and back flat.

►Complete one breath for each repetition of an exercise.

►Exhale during the contraction of the exercised muscle group and inhale during its relaxation.

►Avoid arching the neck and back.

►Avoid locking any joint.

►Always maintain good alignment and technique and complete the largest range of motion possible for each exercise.

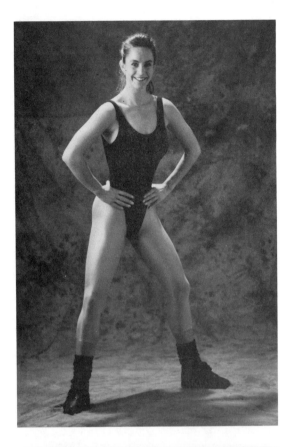

CONDITIONING WORKOUT #1

Squats

▶Keep your feet turned out at a 45 degree angle and slightly more than shoulder width apart. Relax your hips and slowly lower your buttocks toward the floor, going as low as a 90-degree bend in your knees. (Your hips should never go below your knees.) Place your hands on the upper portion of your thighs to help support your back, and avoid bending your knee beyond the line of your toes. Tense your buttocks and thighs and then squeeze yourself back up.

Breathe in as you go down and out as you stand up.

Perform 1-3 sets of 8 repetitions per set. You may take an 8 second rest between sets.

Rear Stationary Lunges

▶Place your feet slightly more than shoulder width apart, both feet pointing in the same direction, one foot in front of the other. Your front foot should be planted with the knee directly above the heel; the other leg is balanced on the ball of the foot. Keep your back heel off the floor for the entire exercise.

Slowly lower yourself toward the floor, dropping your rear knee as low as three inches from the ground.

Avoid bending your front knee beyond the line of the toes of your front foot. Contract your buttocks and thighs to lift yourself back up.

Perform 1-3 sets of 8 repetitions each leg (alternate sides). You may take an 8 second rest between sets.

Calf Raises

▶Place your feet shoulder width apart, hands placed on your hips. Roll through your feet, up onto your toes, lifting both heels off the floor together while contracting your calf muscles.

Perform 1-3 sets of 20-30 repetitions per set. You may take an 8 second rest between sets.

Lateral Shoulder Raises

▶Start with your arms in front of your chest, bent at the elbow at a 90-degree angle. Your forearms should be touching and your palms facing you.

Lift your elbows up at your sides to shoulder height; then bring them back to center.

Perform 1-3 sets of 12 repetitions per set. You may take an 8 second rest between sets.

Shoulder Pull Back

►Start with your arms at shoulder height, bent at the elbow at a 90-degree angle, palms facing downward.

Pull your elbows back, squeezing your shoulder blades together behind you.

Perform 1-3 sets of 12 repetitions per set. You may take an 8 second rest between sets.

Shoulder Press

▶With your arms at your sides, bend your elbows and turn your fists in at shoulder level.

Extend your arms upward and overhead, turning your fists out.

Perform 1-3 sets of 12 repetitions per set. You may take an 8 second rest between sets.

Chest Crosses

▶Raise your arms to shoulder level with your palms facing the floor and elbows bent at 90 degrees.

Squeeze your arms toward the center of your body, crossing one elbow over the other, alternating upper and lower elbows.

Perform 1-3 sets of 12 repetitions per set. You may take an 8 second rest between sets.

Concentrated Chest Press-Up

▶Raise your arms to chest level with your elbows bent at 90 degrees, forearms placed together at the midline of your body with your palms facing upward.

Press your fists upward, contracting the chest muscles, and then lower back down.

Perform 1-3 sets of 12 repetitions per set. You may take an 8 second rest between sets.

Basic Hip Lift—Outer Thigh Abduction

▶Lie on one side, keeping both your top and bottom legs bent.

▶Lift your top leg directly upward, keeping the hips parallel, and lower back down. Be sure that you don't turn your hip as you lift your leg—both of your knees should stay facing directly forward.

Perform 1-3 sets per side of 12 repetitions per set. You may take an 8 second rest between sets.

Basic Hip Lift with Leg Extension— Outer Thigh and Lower Buttocks

▶Perform the basic hip lift, but straighten your top leg after lifting it by extending the heel away from you and squeezing the outer thigh and buttock.

Perform 1-3 sets per side of 12 repetitions per set. You may take an 8 second rest between sets.

Knee Touch to Front with Leg Extension— Outer Thigh and Buttock

►Lie on your side in the basic hip lift position. Drop your top knee to the floor in front of your bottom knee and then straighten and extend your leg to the back, leading with the heel.

Perform 1-3 sets per side of 12 repetitions per set. You may take an 8 second rest between sets.

Basic Inner Thigh Lift (Abduction)

▶Lie on your side with your bottom leg straight and top leg bent. Place the foot of your top leg flat on the floor in front of your bottom leg.

Lift your bottom leg up while keeping the foot flexed and rotating the hip outward. (Point the toes directly forward.) Then lower back down.

Perform 1-3 sets per side of 12 repetitions per set. You may take an 8 second rest between sets.

Full-Range Inner Thigh Lift

▶Perform the same movement as in the basic inner thigh lift, except that after lifting your leg, move it to the rear, bring it back to center and then lower it to the floor.

Perform 1-3 sets per side of 12 repetitions per set. You may take an 8 second rest between sets.

Inner Thigh Knee Squeeze

▶Lie on one side with your top leg bent and foot flat on floor. The bottom leg is bent at the same angle and lies on the floor in front of the top leg.

Lift the knee of the bottom leg up to the knee of the top leg, squeezing the inner thigh, and then lower it back to the floor.

Perform 1-3 sets per side of 12 repetitions per set. You may take an 8 second rest between sets.

Basic Abdominal Crunch

▶Lie on your back, with your feet flat on the floor and knees bent. Place your hands behind your head and keep your elbows open out to your sides. Contract your abdominals and roll your head, shoulders and upper back off the floor. Keep your lower back in contact with the floor at all times. Hold for a second at the top and then roll back down.

Perform 1-3 sets of 12 repetitions per set. You may take an 8 second rest between sets.

Abdominal 3-Level Crunch

►Perform the basic abdominal crunch, except curl up for three counts in three distinct level changes and lower down on the fourth count. Then immediately curl back up again.

Perform 1-3 sets of 12 repetitions per set. You may take an 8 second rest between sets.

Opposite Leg/Cross Arm Abdominal Crunch

▶Start in the basic abdominal crunch position and roll up, reaching your right hand to your left knee and then your left hand to your right knee as you lift a little higher up. Your arms end up crossed at the top position.

Roll back down, uncrossing your arms, to the starting position. Begin the next repetition on the alternate side and continue to alternate through the set.

Perform 1-3 sets of 12 repetitions per set. You may take an 8 second rest between sets.

Oblique Crunch

▶Lie flat on the floor with both knees together. Drop your knees to one side and perform a basic abdominal crunch, lifting your torso toward the ceiling.

Drop your knees to the other side and repeat.

Perform 1-3 sets per side of 12 repetitions per set. You may take an 8 second rest between sets.

Alternating Knee Crunch with Turn

►Starting from the basic crunch position, roll off the floor while turning your upper body to one side and simultaneously bringing your opposite knee in. While turning the body, lead with the shoulder and attempt to connect your shoulder to your opposite knee.

Perform 1-3 sets of 12 repetitions each side per set. You may take an 8 second rest between sets.

Vertical Leg Crunch
with Turn

▶Begin with both legs in the air and knees bent halfway. Make sure your spine is flat along the floor. Curl your shoulders off the floor, attempting to connect your left shoulder to your right knee, and then roll down.

Roll up again and turn to the opposite side, then roll down.

Perform 1-3 sets of 12 repetitions each side per set. You may take an 8 second rest between sets.

Super Crunch

▶Start with both feet in the air, knees halfway bent and toes pointing up. Make sure your back is flat on the floor. Roll your head and shoulders straight up off the floor while simultaneously bringing your knees in.

Extend your legs while rolling back down.

Perform 1-3 sets of 12 repetitions per set. You may take an 8 second rest between sets.

CONDITIONING WORKOUT #2

Biceps Curl

▶Perform this exercise one arm at a time, adding resistance with the other arm. Tuck your elbow of your working arm into your waist, and straighten your arm in front of your body with your palm facing upward. Place the hand of the opposite arm on the forearm and apply resistance while performing the bicep curl. Raise the forearm all the way to the chest and lower.

Complete the set and repeat on the other side.

Perform 1-3 sets each arm of 8 repetitions per set. You may take an 8 second rest between sets.

Triceps Extension

►Lean your upper body slightly forward and place your arms by your sides, with the elbows bent at 90 degrees. Lift your elbows up behind you.

Contract your triceps and extend your forearms to the back, straightening your arms but not locking your elbows. Return to the starting position and repeat.

Perform 1-3 sets of 12 repetitions per set. You may take an 8 second rest between sets.

Wide Grip Back Row

▶Begin with your arms at shoulder height, elbows slightly bent and palms facing each other. Your hands should be shoulder width apart.

Squeeze your shoulder blades together and pull your elbows to the back. Release and spread your back as you bring the arms forward. Concentrate on contracting your back muscles.

Perform 1-3 sets of 12 repetitions per set. You may take an 8 second rest between sets.

Rear Leg Lift—Buttocks

▶Kneel on the floor on your knees and elbows. Keep your head facing downward, in alignment with your spine. Balance on one knee and bend the other at a 90-degree angle with your foot flexed at hip height.

Lift the bent leg to slightly above hip level, contracting the buttocks muscles and being careful to avoid arching your back. Then bring the knee back toward the floor. Keep the foot flexed and the buttocks muscles tight at all times.

Perform 1-3 sets on each leg of 12 repetitions per set. You may take an 8 second rest between sets.

Rear Leg Crossover— Side Buttocks

▶Starting from the rear leg lift position, bring the knee of your working leg in toward your body, crossing it over your opposite leg. Then bring it back to the starting position, leading with your heel.

Perform 1-3 sets on each leg of 12 repetitions per set. You may take an 8 second rest between sets.

Rear Leg Curls— Buttocks

▶Starting from the rear leg lift position, bend the knee of your working leg to 90 degrees so the bottom of the foot is parallel to the ceiling. Extend your leg to a straight line at hip height by flexing the buttocks and extending the hamstring, then curl your leg back to the 90-degree position, contracting your hamstrings.

Perform 1-3 sets on each leg of 12 repetitions per set. You may take an 8 second rest between sets.

Basic Chest Pushups—
Wide Grip

▶Get into a pushup position on the floor, either on your feet or on your knees. For this pushup, place your hands on the floor slightly wider than shoulder width apart. Keep your back flat and your head in line with your spine, tuck in your buttocks and hold in your abdominals. Slowly lower your chest toward the floor and push back up. Avoid locking the elbows when you push back up.

Perform 1 set of 8-12 repetitions per set. You may take a 10-20 second rest between sets.

Narrow Grip Triceps and Chest Pushup

►Use the same pushup position as in the basic pushup, but place your hands on the floor slightly *less* than shoulder width apart. Lower yourself toward the ground, bending your elbows directly to the back, keeping your arms by your sides at all times.

Perform 1 set of 8-12 repetitions per set. You may take a 10-20 second rest between sets.

Diamond Pushup—
Triceps and Chest

▶This is a very advanced pushup. Place your hands on the floor so that your thumbs and index fingers make a diamond shape between your hands. Lower very slowly toward the ground, bending your elbows out to the side, and then push back up. Try this exercise on your knees first, only going down as far as you can handle.

Perform 1 set of 8 repetitions per set. You may take a 10-20 second rest between sets.

Triceps Dip

►Sit on the floor with your feet and palms flat on the floor, both shoulder width apart and pointing in the same direction. Lift your body off the floor by straightening your elbows and then lower back to the floor by bending your elbows. Avoid locking your elbows.

Perform 1-3 sets of 12 repetitions per set. You may take a 10-20 second rest between sets.

Basic Abdominal Crunch

▶Lie on your back, feet flat on the floor and knees bent. Place your hands behind your head and keep your elbows open out to your sides. Contract your abdominals and roll your head, shoulders and upper back off the floor. Keep your lower back in contact with the floor at all times. Hold for a second at the top and then roll back down.

Perform 1-3 sets of 12 repetitions per set. You may take an 8 second rest between sets.

Hold Crunch

▶Start in the basic crunch position on the floor. Roll your head, shoulders and upper back off the floor to the top of your crunch and hold for three counts. Then release on the fourth count.

Perform 1-3 sets of 12 repetitions per set. You may take an 8 second rest between sets.

4-Position Military Crunch

▶Start in the basic crunch position on the floor. Curl up for one count, turn to the side for the second count, turn back to center for the third count, and release on the fourth count. Then repeat on the other side.

Perform 1-3 sets of 12 repetitions per set. You may take an 8 second rest between sets.

Alternating Knee Lift Crunch

▶Start in the basic crunch position. As you curl off the floor, simultaneously bring one knee in towards your chest. This is a straight-up crunch with no turning.

Perform 1-3 sets of 8 repetitions for each knee per set. You may take an 8 second rest between sets.

Vertical Leg Crunch

▶This is the same as the basic crunch except that your feet are off the floor. Extend your legs straight up, flexing your toes slightly in. Keep your knees slightly bent and lift your upper body towards your knees, contracting your lower and upper abdominals.

Perform 1-3 sets of 12 repetitions per set. You may take an 8 second rest between sets.

Weightlifting Workouts

Strength training means using barbells, dumbbells, resistance machines and your own body weight to increase your muscle strength. Years ago, weight training was considered "men's exercise," but that myth no longer applies. Women who weight train—and I'm not referring to bodybuilders per se—have discovered that working with weights makes them slimmer, firmer, stronger and more attractive-looking than just doing aerobic exercise alone.

And it doesn't take long. Most people who take up weight training start seeing very noticeable differences in their bodies in six to ten weeks.

After age twenty, if we don't exercise and keep our muscles active, we begin gradually losing our muscle mass. Since most people who are inactive weigh more in their later years than they did at twenty, the conclusion is simple—they've replaced a lot of their muscle with fat.

Notice that I didn't say that their muscle has turned to fat, because muscle can never turn to fat and fat can't turn to muscle. But muscle can be maintained and rebuilt and fat can be burned off at any age.

Muscular strength exercises are the fastest and quickest way to reshape, build, strengthen and tighten all the major muscle groups of the body, helping you get that fit and lean look. These exercises are very effective in improving your overall appearance and posture as well as providing

> *Muscle can be maintained and rebuilt and fat can be burned off at any age.*

important long term benefits including increased bone mass, improved body composition (less body fat), better posture and decreased risk of injury. Many studies also show cardiovascular benefits from weight training, such as lower blood pressure and lower resting heart rate, as well as improvements in cholesterol levels.

That first benefit, increased bone mass, is one that all of us need to be more concerned about as we age. Women especially are prone to osteoporosis, or loss of bone mass, as they get older. In anyone, loss of bone mass leads to the increased possibility of bone fractures. Strength training can definitely reduce your risk of that problem.

How does weight training decrease your risk of injury? The muscles of the body are like shock absorbers, taking the pounding that the body gets each day. Stronger muscles can better protect ligaments, tendons, bones and joints from everyday wear and tear.

Here's some news that may persuade you to take up strength training: Studies have shown an effect from weightlifting called "caloric afterburn." Muscles that are exercised consume calories for fuel, and it turns out that muscles continue to burn calories even after exercise is completed. So the more muscle you have, the more calories you are burning *even at rest*. Muscle, unlike fat, is a very active tissue that requires 50 to 100 calories per day per pound of muscle just to sustain itself. The best fitness results come from *combining* aerobic exercise and strength training for a strong heart, healthy lungs, low body fat, and lots of lean muscle mass.

About Spot Reducing

You've probably heard it by now—there is no way that you can spot reduce. There is no possible way to get tight, defined abdominal muscles just by doing a million sit-ups when those abdominal muscles are covered with a layer of fat. You'll get the muscle, all right, but you'll never be able to see it until you shed some body fat. This means following a low-fat diet and doing aerobic exercise as well as strength training. The same principle applies to every part of your body: If the backs of your arms are flabby, you can tone the muscle underneath but you've also got to lose the fat on top. And fat loss never happens in one place—it happens simultaneously all over the body.

How to Work Out

Apply the overload principle to your training. The only way to train a muscle is to place a load on it, and as your muscles get stronger, you must place heavier loads. If you want to keep improving your strength, you must increase the weight. But don't increase it until you can do ten repetitions of any exercise in slow, controlled, proper form. Keep a log of your workouts so you know where you stand and how you've progressed. Keep track of the number of repetitions, the amount of weight, and the exercise performed.

Avoid any fast or sudden movements. Strength training should consist of very slow and controlled motion. Never hold your breath for more than a second or two; breathe rhythmically with all your movements. Generally, you want to exhale as you do the work, such as when you raise the bicep curl or rise up from the squat. Then inhale as you release the weight or resistance. Holding your breath while you lift weights is not recommended because of the resulting increase in blood pressure.

Warm up before you work out, and cool down and stretch afterwards. You can do the Warm-up Routine on page 61 and the Cool-Down Routine on page 97, or to be thoroughly warmed before you strength train, you might want to combine your cardiovascular and strength workouts. Do your aerobic workout first and then lift weights.

The Terminology

A repetition or "rep" is a full cycle of any one exercise, such as one bicep curl or one push-up. A set is a group of repetitions performed continually. Generally, you will do one to three sets of each exercise, with between 8 and 12 repetitions per set.

You'll need to try using different size weights in each separate weight lifting exercise until you find a weight that you can lift approximately 12 times without exhaustion, with good form and without rest between repetitions. For every exercise you do, that weight amount is going to be different, so this takes some trial and error.

I suggest you always go for a lighter weight rather than a heavier weight at first. This is called the "reverse pyramid" training principle. In my training, I do three sets per exercise, on the average. The first set is always my warm-up set (even though I've already completed my 5 to 10 minute general warm-up before touching a weight) and I perform 12 to 15 repetitions in this set. My second set is my working set. I pick up a heavier weight than the warm-up set and try to do ten repetitions. My third set is my challenge set, and I try to perform seven to eight repetitions on this set.

So, just like in my routine, you want to form a pyramid with your weightlifting sets:

heaviest - 8 reps

heavy - 10 reps

lightest - 12 reps

The most important element in weight training is maintaining correct posture and good strict form in your movement, in which only the muscles that are working are contracting. If the weight you are using causes you to compromise your form, it is too heavy. Never work your muscles beyond their ability to train with perfect form. The main problems to watch out for in all exercises are the locking of joints, arching of the lower back, and jerking or fast movements.

It will take the body six to twelve weeks to adjust to a specific workout phase before you are ready to move on to the next phase. Once you reach the phase you want, you may wish to maintain it for a longer period of time. For example, if your goal is to get to the intermediate level, you may want to stay at Phase 2 for a long time without moving up to Phase 3. Then all you have to do is vary your workout occasionally but with the intensity of an intermediate exerciser.

Workout Phase 1

Phase 1 of your workout is the foundation building phase. It lasts 6 to 12 weeks, during which you work out two to three times per week, for example on Monday, Wednesday and Friday or Monday and Thursday. You will work only the major muscle groups (legs, chest, back and abdominals).

> *It will take the body six to twelve weeks to adjust before you are ready to move on to the next phase.*

Start with one to two exercises per muscle group and one to two sets per exercise with 10 to 12 repetitions per set. Maintain this basic program for several weeks. As you progress, increase the number of sets and the number of exercises per muscle group. As you get toward the end of Phase 1 (probably eight to ten weeks into the program), you should have increased your program to a three times per week workout with two to three differ-

ent exercises per muscle group and with two to three sets per exercise.

You will be using the "reverse pyramid" training principal, meaning that you increase the amount of weight as you reduce the number of repetitions. (First 12 repetitions, then 10, then 8.) Your first set is your warm-up set (use your light weight), in which you perform 12 to 15 repetitions. Your second set is your working set (use your medium weight) and you should perform 10 to 12 repetitions. Your third set is your challenge set. You should use a little heavier weight than the previous set, but you should never go for a weight that is heavier than your ability to lift it eight to ten times with good form and in total control.

Workout Phase 2

Phase 2 consists of a 6 to 12 week intermediate program. Now that you've established a foundation and built up your strength and endurance working the major muscle groups for a period of time, you can start working on the smaller and more specific muscle groups such as calves, biceps, triceps and shoulders.

This is where we introduce the split routine principal to the workout. The split routine allows you to intensify and specify your workouts, making sure that you don't overwork any specific muscle group by allowing the worked muscles enough rest and recuperation time before they are worked again.

The first workout of the week is a complete workout from Phase 1 (two to three exercises per muscle group, three sets per exercise, doing 12, 10, and then 8 reverse pyramid repetitions).

The second workout of the week is Workout 1 of the split routine workout. Since you are now introducing work on specific muscle groups, you should start on the new exercises with a reduced amount of sets until you get a few workouts under your belt. Start the split routine with one to two exercises per muscle group and work up to two to three exercises per muscle group.

The third workout of the week is Workout 2 of the split routine workout.

Always start the workout by working the major muscle groups first—the legs, chest, back and abdominals. The secondary muscle groups are shoulders, biceps, triceps, forearms and calves. If you start your workout with the smaller muscle groups, you won't be able to work the larger ones adequately because you will already be fatigued. For example, if you first do barbell curls for the biceps (small muscle group) and then try to do bench presses for the chest muscles (large muscle group), the limiting factor will be your fatigued arms.

You should perform this program three times a week (Monday, Wednesday and Friday). Allow one day of rest in between workouts.

Workout Phase 3

Phase 3 consists of a 6 to 12 week program which is an advanced workout. It involves four workouts per week with two back-to-back split routine workouts. For example:

Monday—Workout I
Tuesday—Workout II
Wednesday—Rest
Thursday—Workout I
Friday—Workout II
Saturday—Rest
Sunday—Rest

When working on an advanced split routine workout four times a week, you should build to the point where you do two to three exercises per muscle group, three sets of each exercise on the reverse pyramid principal (12, 10 and 8 rep-

etitions). The first two workout days should be the heavier challenge days. The second two workout days should be a little lighter. You should also vary the exercises you use on the second two days so that you keep your program fresh and your muscles don't get too accustomed to a specific routine.

For example, if you are doing a chest exercise on Monday (say it's the supine dumbell press), during the next chest workout you might do the chest press exercise on a chest press machine. Although you are working the same muscle group, the grip, the feel and the movement are slightly different. The idea is to have variety in your program.

Please keep in mind that not all weightlifting exercises are described in this book. As you progress, you should learn other exercises so you can alternate and vary your routine.

WEIGHTLIFTING ROUTINE #1
using various machines and free weights

Squats

▶Stand with your feet slightly wider than shoulder width apart, knees slightly bent, toes turned out comfortably. Set the barbell on your shoulders. Keep your back tall and your eyes looking straight ahead.

Relax your hips and slowly lower your buttocks toward the floor, as if you were going to sit in a chair behind you. Your buttocks should not go lower than your knees.

Flex your buttocks and thighs at the bottom of the squat and then slowly rise back up to the standing position. Exhale as you lift up.

Leg Extension

►Select an appropriate weight on the leg extension machine. Check that your spine is resting against the back of the chair.

Extend your legs out to a fully lengthened position, without locking your knees. You should exhale as you extend your legs. Hold the fully extended position for a second, and then slowly lower back down to the starting position.

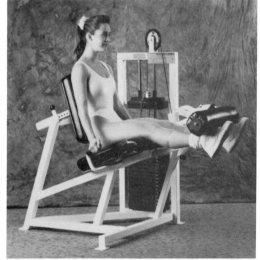

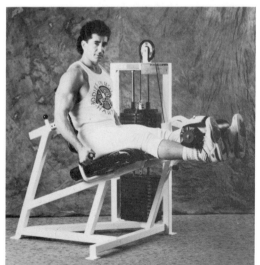

Leg Curl

▶Select an appropriate weight on the leg curl machine. Lying on your stomach, position yourself so your knees are just slightly off the bench.

Bring your heels up as far as you can toward your buttocks, without arching your back or raising your pelvis. Make sure you are able to keep your hips in complete contact with the bench as you raise your heels up. Then slowly lower back down to the starting position. Exhale as you curl your legs up.

Mid-Chest Supine Dumbbell Press

▶Lie on a flat bench with a dumb-bell in each hand and your palms facing upward. The edge of the dumbbell closest to your body should be actually touching your upper chest.

Extend your arms upward until your elbows are straight but not locked, rotating your arms so that your smallest fingers of each hand come toward each other. Keep your spine flat on the bench the entire time. Slowly return to the starting position. Exhale as you extend your arms.

Upper Chest Incline Dumbbell Press

▶Lie on an incline bench in the same starting position as the supine dumbbell press. Extend your arms upward until your elbows are straight but not locked, keeping your palms facing away from your face. Slowly return to the starting position. Exhale as you lift your arms; inhale as you lower them.

The weight you will use on this exercise should be roughly 15% lighter than that used on the supine dumbbell press.

Lower Chest Decline Dumbbell Press

▶Use the same starting position and exertion as in the supine dumbbell press, only perform this exercise while lying on a decline bench.

The weight you will use on this exercise should be roughly 30% lighter than that used on the supine dumbbell press.

Supine Dumbbell Chest Pullover

▶Lie on a flat bench with one dumbbell extended over your chest, holding it in both hands with your thumbs crossed. Keep your elbows slightly bent.

Lower the dumbbell behind your head by lowering your arms and bending your elbows. Make sure you do not lift your buttocks or arch your back off the bench.

Feel a full stretch in your pectoral muscles and then slowly raise the dumbbell to the starting position, right above your chest.

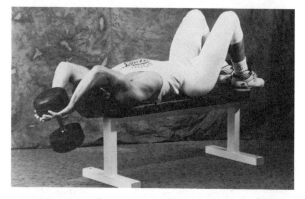

Biceps Curl

▶Stand with your feet slightly wider than shoulder width apart, knees slightly bent, holding an appropriate barbell. Your arms should extend down at your sides, with your palms facing away from your body.

Keeping your elbows and arms close to your sides and your wrists slightly bent, bend your elbows slowly until the weight reaches your upper chest. Slowly lower the weight back to the starting position. Exhale as you lift the weight, inhale as you release it.

Seated Dumbell Curl

▶ Sit on the edge of a flat bench with your back tall and your shoulders relaxed, holding an appropriate dumbbell in each hand.

Keeping your arms close to your sides, slowly curl one dumbbell up toward your shoulder, then slowly return it to your side. Repeat on the other side. Remember to flex your biceps muscle on the upward movement.

Standing Hammer Curl

▶Stand with your feet slightly wider than shoulder width apart, knees slightly bent, holding one dumbbell in each hand, palms facing toward your hips.

Slowly curl one weight toward your shoulder, making sure that your palms remain facing your hips. (You are curling with your thumb coming toward your shoulder.) Slowly lower the weight to the starting position and repeat on the other side.

Forearm Curl

▶ Straddle the middle of a flat bench, holding an appropriate barbell. Lean from your hips (make sure your back is straight) until the backs of your forearms rest on the bench. Your wrists should rest at the edge of the bench, with your palms holding the barbell off the edge of the bench.

Keeping your forearms flat on the bench, curl your wrists toward you and then release.

Exhale as you curl in and inhale as you return to the starting position.

Abdominal Leg Raises

▶Support your forearms on a
Roman chair, with your spine flat
against the back support, keeping
your upper body nice and tall.

Slowly lift your knees to about
waist level, without swinging your
body, and then lower back down.
Exhale as you lift and inhale as
you lower.

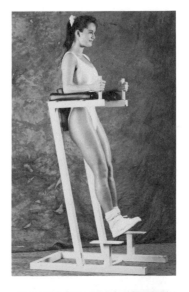
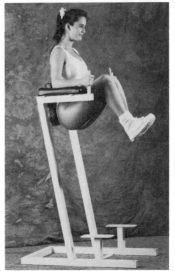

WEIGHTLIFTING ROUTINE #2
using various machines and free weights

Standing Calf Raises

▶Place the balls of your feet on the block of the standing calf machine. Drop your heels below the block so that they are a few inches lower than your toes. Your feet may be in a parallel position, or rotated slightly inward or outward. Each position works the muscle from a slightly different angle.

With your knees slightly bent, rise up on your toes through your full range of motion, as high as you can go. Hold for one second and then slowly lower back down to the starting position. Exhale as you lift and inhale as you lower.

Seated Calf Raises

▶Sit with your back upright on the seated calf machine, with the balls of your feet on the block and the pads resting above your knees.

Slowly rise up on your toes, and then lower down until your heels are below the block and a few inches lower than your toes.

Exhale as you lift up and inhale as you lower.

Donkey Calf Raises

▶Rest your forearms on the pads of the "donkey" machine, with your torso bent from the hips and the balls of your feet resting on the block.

Start with your heels below the block, and then rise up as high as you can on your toes, working through your full range of motion. Slowly lower back down and repeat.

Exhale as you lift up and inhale as you lower.

Lat Pull-Downs— Upper Back

▶ Sit with a tall spine and take a wide grip on the overhead bar. Pull it down toward your chest, with your head looking upward. Then slowly return the weight to the starting position.

Exhale as you pull the weight in and inhale as you release back up.

Seated Rows—Back

▶Sit with your knees bent and feet about shoulder-width apart on the pads. Gripping the rowing handles, keep your chest and head up and then lean forward and row back.

You should go through your full range of motion, bringing the rowing handles all the way in to your waist and then lengthening out until your arms are straight. Be very careful to keep your lower back tall and straight during this exercise.

Exhale as you pull the weight towards you. Inhale as you release back to the starting position.

Bent Over One Arm Row—Back

►Kneel with your left knee on the bench and your right foot on the floor. Your right knee should be slightly bent. Hold a dumbbell in your right hand and extend your arm in a straight line. Keep your spine and neck flat and aligned, with your eyes on the bench.

Slowly bring the dumbbell up toward your waist by bending your elbow, keeping your arm close to your body. Then lower back down and repeat. Be sure not to turn your torso while you lift the weight—make sure your upper body stays stationary. Repeat on the other side.

Exhale as you pull the weight towards you and inhale as you release it.

Seated Dumbbell Shoulder Press

▶Sit on a flat bench with a dumbbell in each hand. For the starting position, place the dumbbells on your thighs and use your thighs to raise the weights to shoulder height. (Raise your knee toward your chest to lift the weight.)

Then slowly raise both arms over your head until they are fully extended, rotating your palms outward and away from you as you lift.

Slowly lower back to the starting position, rotating your palms to face toward you again.

Exhale as you press upwards and inhale as you release back down.

Standing Lateral Flyes— Side Shoulders

▶Stand with your feet shoulder-width apart, knees slightly bent and shoulders relaxed. Hold a dumbbell in each hand (palms facing away from you), directly in front of your hips.

Extend your arms outward and upward until the dumbbells reach shoulder height. Your palms will now be facing toward the floor. Slowly return to the starting position.

Exhale as you lift outward and inhale as you release back to the starting position.

Bent-Over Lateral Flyes (Back of Shoulders)

▶Sit on the edge of a bench with a dumbbell in each hand. Bend over so that your chest is on your thighs, your face is parallel to the floor, and the weights are underneath your knees. Your palms should be facing each other and your elbows should be slightly bent.

Extend your arms outward until the dumbbells are at shoulder height. Your palms should turn outward as you lift, so that in the top position they are facing behind you. Slowly lower back to the starting position.

Exhale as you lift outward and inhale as you release back to the starting position.

Triceps Extension

►Lie on a flat bench with a barbell held over your shoulders with fully extended arms. Your palms should face away from you.

Slowly bend your elbows as far you can until the barbell goes past your forehead and out of your eyesight. Then slowly bring the barbell back to the starting position. Make sure that your upper arms stay stationary and keep your elbows at a set distance from each other. (Don't let them open outwards.)

Exhale as you lift the barbell upward and inhale as you exhale back down.

Standing Triceps Extension

▶Stand with your feet shoulder-width apart, gripping a triceps bar with an overhand grip (palms facing down). Your elbows should be bent in a 90-degree angle in the starting position, forearms parallel to the floor.

Keeping your body stationary, push down on the triceps bar until your arms are fully extended, without locking your elbows. Slowly release back up.

Exhale as you push down and inhale as you release back up.

Overhead Triceps Extension

▶Sit on the edge of a flat bench with your back tall, eyes looking straight ahead. Grip one dumbbell overhead on your flat palms, with your thumbs and forefingers in a diamond shape.

Slowly bend your elbows, lowering the weight behind your head as low as you can comfortably go. Then raise back up to the fully extended position without locking your elbows. Keep your elbows close to your head through the entire range of movement.

Exhale as you press the dumbbell upward and inhale as you release the dumbbell back down.

Abdominal Leg Raises

▶Lie on an inclined sit-up bench, with your head on the high side and your feet on the low side, pressing your spine flat on the bench. Start with your knees bent halfway and raised just above your hips.

Contract the lower abdominal muscles and bring your knees upward toward your chest, so your feet rise higher in the air. Then slowly release back to the starting position. Stay very controlled through this exercise—do not swing or arch your lower back.

Exhale as you bring your knees toward your chest and inhale as you lower your knees back down.

Abdominal Curl

▶Lie on an inclined situp bench, with your head on the low side and your feet on the high side, knees bent and feet curled around the padded bar.

Cross your arms in front of your chest and curl up to a half-way sitting position. Slowly lower down and repeat.

Exhale as you lift upwards and inhale as you lower yourself back toward the starting position.

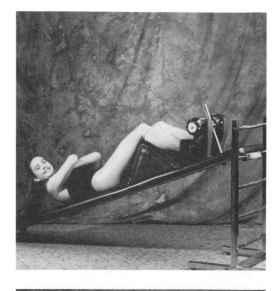

Walking
Running
Sprinting

Although running reached its peak of popularity in the 1970s and early 1980s, running as a sport and exercise is nothing new. In fact, early hieroglyphics show men running, and running races were documented in the first Olympic games held in 776 B.C. Running as exercise appeals to many people because of its efficiency—in a short time, you get great cardiovascular benefits, strong muscular legs, and quick calorie expenditure.

But don't forget that there is more than one kind of running. When most people think of starting a running program, they think of long-distance running for cardiovascular fitness, or maybe entering a 5-K or 10-K race or even a marathon. But short distance running or speed training is a terrific form of fitness training that many people overlook. In fact, I see many people running long-distance who would be better off sprinting or speed training—their bodies are naturally built for speed, not distance. Of course, even sprinters build up at least a moderate base of endurance training before launching into a speed program. In this chapter, we'll review both types of running.

> *Walking and running can produce the same cardiovascular benefits and will burn the same number of calories.*

If You're a Beginner

If you're a beginner to exercising, or if you are more than fifteen pounds overweight, you don't want to go outside and just start running. In fact, I would recommend that you go outside and start walking instead. Walking and running can produce the exact same cardiovascular benefits and will burn the same number of calories. The only difference is that with walking, you have to be out there longer. Runners can have a great workout in half an hour of running, while walkers would probably have to walk briskly for about an hour to get the same results.

The following is a 12-week progressive walking program designed for beginners who want to improve their cardiovascular fitness. If you have been exercising previously, you may want to begin this program at Week 5 and then work up from there. Remember, a good walking program can provide you with all the cardiovascular fitness necessary for a healthy life. If you feel you want a greater fitness level than this workout provides, master this routine first and then progress to the running workout that follows. And with this workout, as with any workout, begin with the Warm-up and Stretch Routine (page 61) and end with the Cool-down Routine (page 97). Along with warming up, walking and cooling down, I also suggest that you do the Progressive Flexibility Routine (page 109) at least two times per week.

WEEK — **Walking Phase 1**

1 **MON, WED, FRI**
Walk 20 minutes—Comfortable pace

2 **REPEAT WEEK 1**

3 **MON, WED, FRI**
Walk 30 minutes—Comfortable pace

4 **REPEAT WEEK 3**

WEEK — Walking Phase 2

5 MON

Walk 30 minutes—Brisk pace
WED

Walk 30 minutes—Comfortable pace
FRI

Walk 30 minutes—Brisk pace

6 REPEAT WEEK 5

7 MON

Walk 30-40 minutes—Brisk pace
WED

Walk 45 minutes—Comfortable pace
FRI

Walk 30-40 minutes—Brisk pace

8 REPEAT WEEK 7

WEEK — Walking Phase 3

9 MON, FRI

Walk 30-40 minutes—Brisk pace
WED, SAT OR SUN

Walk 45 minutes—Comfortable pace

10 REPEAT WEEK 9

11 MON, FRI

Walk 40 minutes—Brisk pace
WED, SAT OR SUN

Walk 50 minutes—Comfortable pace

12 MON, WED, FRI

Walk 45-50 minutes—Brisk pace
SAT OR SUN

Walk 60 minutes—Comfortable pace

Moving On

If you're past the beginning exerciser stage, but you've never run before, I recommend you start with a mixed program of running and walking. Find a fairly flat path to follow; hill running will come later. Walk first to warm up, starting slowly and then increasing your pace after about five minutes. Then, when you feel warm and ready, jog a few blocks. When you start to feel winded, slow your pace to a brisk walk again. Keep this run/walk pattern going for twenty minutes, and then slow to a walk for a cool-down for the last five minutes.

At first, you may be walking briskly more than you are running. When you run, you should run slowly, paying attention to your good posture and your breathing. Think of landing lightly on your feet. There should be no tension in your shoulders, and they should be dropped and relaxed. Avoid making a fist with your hands—keep them relaxed as well. Breathe naturally and easily, remembering to exhale and push the air out of you. Always pay attention to how your body feels; this is the only way to know when you should be walking and when you should be running.

The following workout routine is designed for the beginner or intermediate exerciser who wishes to develop a greater level of cardiovascular fitness than that provided by the walking workout. As I stated before, a good walking program will give you all the cardiovascular fitness necessary for a healthy life, but this program will take you beyond that.

The routine also incorporates other forms of cardio-

If you're past the beginning exerciser stage, start with a mixed program of running and walking.

vascular exercise besides running and walking, such as aerobics classes, Stairmaster programs, swimming, etc. I call this *cardio crosstraining,* and on cardio crosstraining days you can choose your own way to work out aerobically. I also recommend that you do conditioning workouts for greater muscular balance.

The goal of this routine is to take you to the level of being able to complete 5-10 kilometer fitness runs in your local area. If you wish to be competitive in these runs, however, you should also do the Speed Workout (page 199), in order to build your speed.

Remember, with this or any workout, begin with the Warm-up and Stretch Routine and end with the Cool-down Routine. You should also do the Progressive Flexibility Routine twice per week.

WEEK Walk/Run Phase 1

1 MON, WED, FRI

Walk 20 minutes—Comfortable pace

2 MON, WED, FRI

Walk 30 minutes—Comfortable pace

3 MON, FRI

Walk 30 minutes—Brisk pace
WED

Walk 35 minutes—Comfortable pace

4 MON, FRI

Walk 30 minutes—Brisk pace
WED

Walk 35 minutes—Comfortable pace
SAT OR SUN

Cardio crosstrain—Easy to moderate pace—30-45 minutes

WEEK Walk/Run Phase 2

5 MON, FRI

Run 10/Walk 20 minutes—Comfortable pace
WED

Walk 30-40 minutes—Brisk pace
SAT OR SUN

Cardio crosstrain—Easy to moderate pace—30-45 minutes

6 MON, FRI

Run 15/Walk 15 minutes—Comfortable pace
WED

Walk 30-40 minutes—Brisk pace
Conditioning Workout #1
SAT OR SUN

Cardio crosstrain—Easy to moderate pace—30-45 minutes

7 MON, FRI

Run 20/Walk 10 minutes—Comfortable pace
WED

Walk 45 minutes—Brisk pace
Conditioning Workout #2
SAT OR SUN

Cardio crosstrain—Easy to moderate pace—40-50 minutes

8 SAME AS WEEK 7

Moving Forward with Long Distance Running

If you've successfully completed phases 1, 2 and 3 of the running program, you may want to move on. Or you may not—many people continue running programs like this one for life and have incredible health benefits to show for it. But if you are interested in training your body to run greater distances or faster times, four to six months into your program may be a good time to do it.

One word of warning, though. It is unwise even for very fit runners to increase their mileage too quickly. Current research shows that unless you are training for a marathon or another distance-running competitive event, it's advisable to limit your running to 15 to 20 miles per week. Fifteen to twenty miles a week of running is enough to provide you with a fit body and good health. More than that and you significantly increase your chances of injury. Of course, some well-trained runners regularly run 30 to 50 miles a week with no harm.

Also, as you begin to increase your mileage, keep in mind that it takes your muscles about three weeks to adapt to any new training program. So if you've been running only 12 miles a week, and now you are going to start running 16 miles a week, your body is going to take about three weeks to adapt. This is true even though you may feel strong and assume your body has adapted sooner. So don't increase your mileage or the intensity of your workouts more often than every three weeks.

If you want to increase your distance or your speed, you may want to start running more than three days a week. As with all changes in your body's routine, make the change gradually. If you are going to stay within the 15- to 20-mile-per-week limit, you probably won't run more than four days a week.

WEEK Walk/Run Phase 3

9 MON

Run 30/Walk 10 minutes
Conditioning Workout #1

WED

Run 30/Walk 10 minutes

FRI

Cardio crosstrain—30-45 minutes
Conditioning Workout #2

SAT OR SUN

Run/Walk 45 minutes

10 MON, WED, FRI

Same as Week 9

SAT OR SUN

Run/Walk 50 minutes

11 MON

Run 30/Walk 15 minutes
Conditioning Workout #1

WED

Run 30/Walk 15 minutes

FRI

Cardio crosstrain—45 minutes
Conditioning Workout #2

SAT OR SUN

Run/Walk 50-60 minutes

12 MON, WED, FRI

Same as Week 11

SAT OR SUN

Run/Walk 50-60 minutes

Try not to run four days consecutively—split them up throughout the week. Also, you want to alternate long runs and short runs, so that you aren't running exactly the same mileage every day. A long or hard running day should always be followed by a short or easy running day, or a rest day. A sample four-day schedule might look like this:

Monday—4 miles
Tuesday—3 miles
Thursday—4 miles
Saturday—5 miles
Total—16 miles

If you really get into running and decide to run five days a week, be sure that those five days are non-consecutive, and alternate long and short runs. I do not recommend that anyone run more than five days a week. If you want to exercise more than five days a week, you should do something besides running on the sixth day, just to give your body the benefits of cross-training, and on the seventh day you should take a complete rest.

A sample five-day running schedule might look like this:

Monday—3 miles
Tuesday—2 miles
Wednesday—5 miles
Friday—4 miles
Sunday—6 miles
Total—20 miles

As you can see in both the five-day and four-day workouts, one day each week is devoted to a

All you need to get started on a running program is a little will, a little enthusiasm and a good pair of running shoes. Running is easy because no matter where you are, you can always find a place to do it. Remember, though, that during a run various elements can change on you. It's important to be able to shift gears accordingly. I always look for a running course that has a soft surface like grass, dirt or the sand on the beach. But the road will do, too. Knowing how to adjust for different surfaces during a run and having good shoes will help you make your runs safe and effective. For example:

UPHILL
To adjust to the difficulty of climbing, shorten your stride and lift your knees a little higher. Lean your body slightly forward.

DOWNHILL
To control downhill momentum, lean back slightly and plant your heels softly into the ground. Bring your elbows further back during the stride.

SAND
To keep your pace and to minimize sinking into the sand, shorten your stride and quicken your pace a little.

ROAD
To lessen the impact of the hard surface, try to glide a little more, lengthening your stride and keeping your feet closer to the ground throughout the stride.

UNEVEN GROUND (grass, dirt, etc.)
To adjust to surprises on this course, such as uneven grass or an unseen dip in the dirt, run with your knees slightly bent. This will keep your balance in case you get caught off guard.

TRAFFIC
To maintain safety, run on the opposite side of the street so you face the oncoming traffic. Keep your eyes on the road.

DARK
Don't try new courses unless they are well lit. When running on familiar off-road courses, keep your knees slightly bent through the stride to prepare for possible uneven ground.

Buying Running Shoes

▶ Running shoes should be replaced every 400 miles or so.

▶ If you go to a running shoe store, have a salesperson look at the soles of a pair of your exercise shoes. From the wear patterns on them, he or she can make recommendations of the type of shoe you should buy. If your shoes tend to wear along the outside, you need a shoe with good flexibility and cushioning. If your shoes tend to wear on the inside, you need a more rigid, stable shoe.

▶ Running shoes come in two basic shapes—curved and straight. If you look at the soles of running shoes, curved shoes will have more of an hourglass shape to them, while straight shoes do not have a curvy cut-out around the arch—the soles appear as simple ovals. Try on both kinds to see which feels right. Ideally, you are trying to best match the shape of your foot.

▶ Try shoes on in the afternoon, as your feet swell during the day. Your feet will swell when they run.

▶ Make sure you have a little room at the toe—about one-half inch. As long as the shoe fits correctly around the middle of your foot, don't be afraid to leave a little toe room.

▶ Make sure you wear socks of the same thickness you run in when you try on shoes.

▶ Move around when you are trying on shoes. Run in place.

▶ Break in your shoes by wearing them for your daily activities for a day or two before you try to run in them.

longer run. This is a good practice to get you out of the rut of running approximately the same mileage every day, and also to build your endurance beyond a few miles. As you get stronger, you may want to increase this one-day-a-week run to a longer distance such as seven or eight miles. This will give you the benefit of having one long endurance day without significantly increasing your weekly mileage.

Hill Training

Hills can strengthen your running body, which has already built up endurance from running 15 to 20 miles a week. Running hills will strengthen all the large muscles of the legs—quadriceps, hamstrings and calves—which will in turn strengthen your knees and ankles. With a small amount of hill training built into your running program, you will build both endurance and speed. Training on hills allows you to shift your weight farther forward on your feet and to use your ankles for a stronger push. It also pushes your cardiovascular system to work harder than it would on flat runs.

Hill training is much harder than flat running, however. It is recommended that you begin hill training on a moderate grade of about 10 to 15 percent, and that you only hill train one day out of the week.

Training for a 5-K Run

One way to vary your training program and also to have some fun is to enter your first race. "What?" you say. "But I've only been running for six months!" True, but you've been regularly running three miles at a time, and three miles is very close to the distance of one of the most exciting races there is—the 5-K (3.1 miles). It's a short race that gives you all the excitement of competition.

In fact, if you already feel comfortable running three miles, you can train for a 5-K race in about six weeks. The training involves learning to pick up your pace when you run, because a 5-K is run at a fairly good clip. Of course, you could just jog through the race, but if you wanted to jog you wouldn't be racing, would you?

To run a solid 5-K, you need both endurance and speed. To reach your best time, you're going to have to run at about 90 percent of your maximum effort the whole time. That is probably not what your body is accustomed to. Remember the difference between aerobic and anaerobic work? When you're out for your normal three-times-a-week fitness runs, you're probably only working at about 50 to 60 percent of your maximum effort. This medium effort is an aerobic workout, which allows you to sustain your runs for fairly long distances without getting exhausted. You're continually taking in just enough oxygen as your muscles need to keep performing.

But anaerobic running is when you push your body beyond the point where you can take in enough oxygen for your working muscles, so you start gasping for air. The advantage of training in this anaerobic state is that it trains your body to work at a more highly stressed level, and it will actually improve your overall cardiovascular performance. Only by pushing your heart and lungs past their aerobic threshold can you raise your aerobic threshold to a higher level. So, in training for the 5-K, you're going to have to start running

To run a solid 5-K, you need both endurance and speed.

faster—at about 80 percent effort—on your training runs. Eighty percent effort is enough to train you for when you will have to give 90 percent. More than 80 percent will just wipe you out.

Okay, so no more 10-minute miles. But instead of just racing out the front door and down the street, you might want to try a more scientific approach: Two days a week, go for "tempo" runs. These runs are like your regular runs, but somewhere about halfway through you want to run hard and fast—eighty percent effort—for a period of time.

In the beginning, that period should be only eight to ten minutes. Then add two more minutes of speed running every week or ten days. Eventually you want to work your way up to sixteen minutes of speed running in the middle of your regular run.

You also want to increase your strength for speed running. Use the weight training program in the previous chapter to strengthen your quadriceps and hamstrings.

Running small hills is also great for strengthening your legs—I recommend you run up and walk down. The downhill is what causes the wear and tear on your joints. Taking a step class at a health club or aerobics class will also help strengthen the power in your legs.

You should also include one day per week of distance running in your 5-K training. Remember that the 5-K requires both endurance and speed. Keep in mind that distance running in training for a 5-K is not LONG distance. One five- or six-mile run a week should be plenty of mileage, in addition to your two "tempo" runs and your strength training workout.

So let's say you're training four days a week for the 5-K. A sample first week of training might look something like this:

Monday—regular 30-minute run (plus 10 more minutes for walking warm-up and cool-down), plus 20 minutes of strength training for the legs
Wednesday—tempo run with 10 minutes of speed running in a total 30-minute run (plus ten more minutes for walking warm-up and cool-down)
Friday—tempo run with 10 minutes of speed running in a total 30-minute run (plus ten more minutes for walking warm-up and cool-down)
Sunday—5-mile run plus 20 minutes of strength training for legs

On Race Day

Be prepared for the odd feeling of running faster than you've run before. You must be thoroughly warm before you start, so be sure to jog for 10 minutes or so and do the stretches in the Warm-Up Routine (page 61). Make sure that you stretch your hamstrings and calves thoroughly. Then keep moving right up until it's time to line up for the race. Jogging in place is fine.

When the gun goes off, don't give it all out effort right away. The best strategy for the three miles of the 5-K is to run quickly and efficiently for the first mile, relax a bit on the second mile, and then give your hardest effort on the final mile. A lot of people, even experienced competitors, blow the race by going too hard on the first mile, and then feeling spent too soon.

It's always a good idea to find someone who is running at a pace that looks good to you and go with them. Then, in the final mile, try to pass them.

After the finish line, keep jogging at a slower pace for 5 to 10 minutes to cool down. Don't skip this part of the day, because your body needs to slow down a bit after working that hard before coming to a complete stop.

Running for Speed

The other important form of running, running short distances for speed, is often overlooked in our recent love-affair with the benefits of slow, long-distance running. In fact, many people assume that sprinting and speed running are only for competitive athletes, not for those who run for fitness. Not so. Look around you at all the different body types. Are all those people perfectly built for endurance running? Of course not—there are many different kinds of bodies out there!

In speed training development, there are many variables. Your weight plays an important factor, especially if you are over or underweight. How your strength is distributed and the physiology of your muscle tissue are also determining factors.

Everyone is born with a certain amount of fast-twitch (speed) muscle fibers and a certain amount of slow-twitch (endurance) muscle fibers in the different muscle groups of their bodies. How much of each type of muscle fiber you have is going to determine what kind of natural athlete you are. If you have a greater percentage of fast-twitch muscle fibers in your legs, you are going to be a much more talented sprinter than a marathoner. Pre-conditioning and past conditioning also play a role in maximizing speed.

The bottom line is that everyone can improve his or her speed considerably. It is possible for anyone to gain from several tenths of a second to several seconds in the 100-yard dash. Speed training will also enhance your performance in other sports activities.

Interval training

Interval training, in running or in any other sport, involves alternating high-intensity exertion with slower, recovery exercise. In running, this means sprinting at top speed for a specified length of time or distance, then slow jogging for another specified time or distance, then sprinting again, etc. Interval training consists of several "repetitions" or "reps," combining the fast run and the recovery run. You repeat these repetitions several times, increasing the number of them as you get stronger. Interval training is probably the single best way to improve your running, both in terms of speed and endurance.

Many people confuse interval training with speed training. They are very different, because in speed training you do not repeat an effort until you are completely recovered. In interval training, you never completely recover from a speed effort. Instead you partially recover by jogging or light running and then repeat the effort at regular intervals.

The reason that interval training is so effective is that it forces you to push yourself beyond your normal endurance training range and into an anaerobic state. By placing yourself in this anaerobic state repeatedly but for short intervals, your body will learn to adapt to training beyond its aerobic threshold. This trains your heart to work at higher levels than what it previously could, so the end result is that you are able to run faster all the time. To achieve the best results from interval training, you have to keep the recovery period short.

Interval training is recommended for attaining faster speeds as well as increasing your aerobic capacity, but it is also useful for training for longer distance speed events such as running distances over 800 meters. Interval training has the double benefit of training you for endurance and speed simultaneously.

How do you set up an interval training program? First, you must choose the distance of your repetition—1/4 mile (440 yards) is a good length if you are running 10K races; 1/8 mile (220 yards) is a good length if you are running a 5K. Then, run that distance slightly faster than the goal pace you are trying to achieve, and jog slowly in between to recover. When you begin interval training, you will probably want to make the recovery distance the same length as the repetition distance. As you get stronger, decrease the recovery distance. Gradually increase the number of repetitions you do.

Fartlek

Fartlek training is a relative of interval training. Fartlek is Swedish for "speed play," and in fartleks, you pick up the tempo of your run for a few minutes, then slow down to recover. It differs from interval training in that it is unstructured—you have no prescribed interval distance or speed. You run according to how you want to run on that particular day. For this reason, fartleks are not ideal for beginners, because they don't allow you to learn pacing and to measure your improvement over specific interval times or distances. For more advanced runners, however, fartleks may be superior to intervals, because they mimic what may happen in an actual race, when you suddenly have to push yourself to pull ahead. Hill fartleks are a popular variation on fartleks. You run at an average pace until you come to a hill, then you accelerate as you go up the hill and slow down to recover as you come down the hill.

Burst Speed

Burst speed is the type of speed you need for very short sprints, such as the 40-yard dash. Burst speed can be improved by sprinting all out for 5 to 15 seconds during every minute of a three-mile run, or by doing pure speed workouts such as the ones that follow. You rest completely between sprints, so that you can run all-out during every effort.

Burst speed workouts are not for beginners. Even experienced runners should work into pure speed workouts, starting their sprint from a running start rather than from a still position. Remember to warm-up thoroughly and stretch thoroughly, and also to strength train the muscles of the legs with weights. The most important strength training exercise for speed development is the squat.

Sprinting/Speed Training Programs

All parts of the introductory program should be executed at no more than 50% effort. This helps to prevent injuries, keeps you from overtraining, and will help you to develop a positive attitude toward your training. You want to start to build up your muscles, not tear them down.

Speed Workout Phase 1

Every time you work out, it is very important to do a complete warm up. Jog 1/2 to 1 mile on a soft surface, then do stretching exercises for 15-20 minutes (see page 61). All stretching should be done slowly and methodically.

Then, on grass or a track with good running shoes, do four to six stride build-ups for 100 yards. Stride build-ups build in speed from slow to fast. When you begin, the speed should not be more than a jog, and then you get progressively faster every time. This exercise is very important because it teaches you how to run fast under control. If you have never run fast or sprinted before, it will take the better part of six months to develop a good running pattern.

Workout # 1

Three to four times—440 yards (one time around the track). Recover completely after each run. This generally takes three to five minutes.

Workout # 2

Ten times—100 yards back and forth (Run 100 yards, slow down, turn around, run back. Do not wait to recover completely before beginning again.)

Workout # 3

Three to four times—200 or 300 yards. Recover completely after each run.

Workout # 4

Three to five times—150 yards. Recover completely after each run.

The first four to eight weeks you should work out at no more than 50% effort. Make sure that you run slowly enough to finish the workout. It is not important how fast you go, but it is important that you complete the workout.

Speed Workout Phase 2

The running exercises in Phase 2 are the same as Phase 1, however you will start challenging yourself as you get in better condition. It is important that you always run within your ability and under control. If you find yourself struggling when you run, slow down a bit because you can't handle that speed in your present condition. Let it happen and don't force it.

In Phase 2, you should start timing your running drills and writing your times down when you finish your workout.

Another important point is always to run in the manner I call "step down." Do each one of your running exercises a little faster than the previous one. For example, run the first four hundred yards at 80 seconds, the next one at 75 seconds, the next at 70 seconds and the final one at 65 seconds. This teaches you to run under control. If you find yourself running faster on the first one, slow down.

Running this way always gives you a gauge on how you are doing and where you are in your conditioning process. If you find you are not progressing after a period of time, back off a little and take a day off. You may be overtraining.

Speed Workout Phase 3

These last 4-8 weeks are your final development stage. You will cut down on the volume and distance of your runs and increase the speed and intensity.

Workout #1

Four times—200 meters "step down." (At this stage, you may also use running shoes with spikes for added speed.) Recover completely after each run.

Workout #2

Ten times—100 yards back and forth. (At this point, your last three or four 100 yards should be all-out or close to all-out effort. Do not wait for full recovery before beginning again.)

Workout #3

Four to six times—100-160 yard accelerations. Recover fully after each run.

Workout #4

Four to six 50-yard dashes at full or close to full speed. Recover fully after each run.

Swimming and Water Aerobics

Swimming involves all of the major muscles in the body, and as a result, provides the body with excellent overall conditioning as well as aerobic benefits. Swimming has the added benefit of being a nearly non-impact exercise with few stress-related injuries, because the buoyancy of water reduces pressure on the joints and bones.

For these and many other reasons, swimming is considered the most popular participation sport in the world. Most people learn to swim at some time in their lives.

If you haven't swum for a while, you may find it easier to begin a swimming program by taking classes at a local swim club, YMCA or city recreation department. The American Red Cross also offers a certificated swimming program at a variety of levels. You may think that you already know how to swim, and you probably do, but some formal lessons or coaching can really make a difference in how efficient you are in the water. You'll find that classes are available for swimmers at all levels of expertise.

If you are a serious fitness swimmer, you might want to consider joining a Masters swimming program, offered at public and private pools around the country. Masters teams offer organized, coached workouts for swimmers of all ages, from 19 to 90 and over, and all skill levels, from beginners to former Olympians. While the focus of Masters swimming is keeping fit, swimmers also have the opportunity to compete in local and national swim meets with other swimmers in their age group.

> *Swimming provides the body with excellent overall conditioning as well as aerobic benefits.*

All you need to start a swimming program is a place to swim and a comfortable swim suit. Most regular swimmers, especially those with longer hair, wear a swim cap to keep their hair out of the way. A pair of plastic eye goggles is also a good idea to help keep your eyes from becoming irritated by pool chemicals. When shopping for goggles, try on several pairs to see what pair best fits the shape of your head and eyes—some people are better off with oval goggles, and others with round ones. Contrary to the manufacturers' claims, all goggles will fog up at some point.

What's the most important thing to keep in mind when you swim? *Always swim in an area protected by a trained lifeguard.* No matter how good you are.

Swimming Laps

Swimming laps is a great form of cardiovascular exercise. However, even people who exercise regularly and think they are in good shape are often surprised to find that they can only swim a few continuous laps of the pool before feeling very out-of-breath. Part of the reason is that swimming, unlike cycling or running, involves working the whole body, and particularly the upper body. Also, more than other exercises, swimming requires the conscious control and coordination of breathing with motion, something that beginning swimmers often find exhausting. However, as you spend more time in the water, your breathing will become as natural in swimming as it is in land-based sports.

When you swim laps, you'll want to know how far you are going. Most recreational pools in the United States, particularly older ones, are 25 yards long, divided into 6 lanes. It takes swimmers about 72 lengths of a 25-yard pool to swim a mile. Most swimming competitions are held in pools built to international standards that are 50 meters long.

There are four main swimming strokes for fitness and competition: freestyle (sometimes called crawl), breaststroke, backstroke and butterfly. Each stroke offers a different, challenging combination of synchronized arm and leg motions and breathing patterns. Although many swimmers naturally excel at one particular stroke, the best way to improve your general level of fitness and become a skillful swimmer, while adding variety to your workout, is to work on all the strokes. This way, all parts of the body get exercised and no one part gets overtrained or fatigued. That is one of the wonderful side benefits of swimming, as opposed to running or cycling or many other exercise sports. The motion changes all the time in swimming—as often as you want it to.

The key to becoming a better swimmer is developing an efficient stroke. If you watch good swimmers, the most striking thing about them is how effortless and natural their stroke is. They don't fight the water, but work with it to move forward. Gaining this kind of efficiency and "water-consciousness" is a matter of experimenting with your stroke as you swim, getting advice from teachers or other swimmers, and of course, practice. One good way to develop an efficient stroke is to concentrate on trying to swim each lap of the pool with a minimum number of strokes. At first, don't concentrate on speed, but on technique. Try to wring the maximum benefit from each stroke. Later, work on swimming faster while maintaining the same number of strokes per length.

Another important element of lap swimming, particularly when trying to swim for distance, is to maintain an even pace and a *consistent* number of strokes per pool length. If your pace slows, or if you find yourself taking more strokes than usual per length, you are tiring out and should adjust your pace.

As you log more swimming hours, both your speed and endurance will improve, partly because you are getting stronger and more fit, and partly because your stroke technique and efficiency are improving. The more you train, the more natural your stroke and consistent your pace will become.

Swimming, like running and cycling and many other aerobic sports, can be an endurance activity or it can be a sprint activity. Either one will strengthen the heart and lungs and improve your overall conditioning. The best way to train your respiratory and cardiovascular systems and realize the maximum benefits of swimming is to combine endurance and speed training. Endurance training consists of swimming long distances at a moderate pace. Speed training consists of swimming repeated sprints of short distances at a high level of effort, with resting periods of variable length between the sprints. But in order to develop any speed at distance swimming, first you must build up a minimal base of endurance swimming. This base can be as short as one mile of continual endurance swimming.

Training Devices

Kickboards, pull-buoys and hand paddles are some of the more common swimming aids

The best way to train in swimming is to combine sprint swimming and lap swimming.

and training devices seen around the pool. Kickboards are great for improving the strength in your leg kicks and your overall fitness. Any swimming stroke can be performed using a kickboard, but because your arms are holding the board, only the legs do the work of the stroke. This develops the large muscle groups of the legs, and gives you a chance to improve the mechanics of your kick.

Styrofoam pull-buoys are used to build overall upper-body strength and improve stroke mechanics. The pull-buoy is held between the legs, so that the lower body is held up without kicking. This forces the upper body to do the whole work of the stroke. Pull-buoys are often combined with hand paddles to greatly overload the work of the upper body.

Hand paddles are used for strengthening arm, shoulder, chest and back muscles, and for improving stroke technique. They essentially enlarge the size of your hand, so you have to work against the increased resistance of a larger "hand" in the water. Paddles are available in a range of sizes. You should choose a size large enough to give you an increased feeling of resistance, but not so large that you can't use them and make it across the pool. Using too large a paddle for a long time can put undue strain on the joints of your shoulder and elbow, so you might want to borrow different pairs from fellow swimmers to test out before buying your own.

> *Even people who exercise regularly are often surprised at how quickly they tire when swimming.*

The Swim Workout

To help you get the most out of your time in the pool, your swim workout should be divided into several components or sets. A good work-out will include at least a warm-up set, a main set, and a cool-down set. As in any aerobic activity, your swim should start with a warm-up, lasting maybe 10 to 20% of the total distance of your workout. Your goal here is to get your blood moving and to limber up your muscles and joints. During your warm-up, you should swim at an easy, comfortable pace. The main set is where the major work of your swim is done. This set could include a combination of long-distance swimming to develop endurance and conditioning, and sprints to develop strength and speed. You should end your workout with a brief cool-down to give your heart and breathing a chance to return gradually to their resting levels.

Swimmers often add other sets to their workout that focus on specific goals. You might add a "drill set" after your warm up, where you concentrate on developing your technique in one stroke. For example, to work on your freestyle stroke, you might try swimming one length of the pool with the right arm only, one with the left only, and then one using the normal two-armed stroke. You'd be surprised at how this kind of drill helps you correct errors and inefficiencies in your stroke.

You may also wish to add a "kick set," in which you kick with a kickboard to develop your legs. Advanced swimmers often include a "pull set" where they swim with hand paddles and pull-buoys to develop upper-body strength and stroke technique.

You'll find that your swim workout will be more challenging and fun if it has a goal. For example, a beginner's goal might be "I will swim eight lengths of freestyle without stopping," while an advanced swimmer might have a goal like "I will swim ten 100-yard sprints in under 75 seconds." Adding such a challenge to your workout and then meeting your goal is a good way to improve as a swimmer, but it is important to keep your goals realistic, especially at first.

By varying your pace, strokes and breathing, and breaking your workout into sets with specific goals, you can keep the fun in swimming and get a great workout too.

A Beginner's Program

As I've said, even people who exercise regularly are often surprised at how quickly they tire when swimming. So be easy on yourself when you start a swimming program. Like every other kind of exercise, look for small improvements. The best way to do this is to keep records of how many laps you swam and what your time was for various distances.

Improvement comes fairly quickly in swimming—the lungs and circulatory system, as well as the large muscle groups of the arms and legs, will adapt well to the new stresses that swimming puts on them. As a beginning-level swimmer, your swimming log will probably show measurable improvement every four to six weeks of your swimming program, assuming that you swim at least three times a week.

The first thing you must do as a new swimmer is build up a base of endurance swimming. From this base, you can then work on your speed. A good first goal for a new swimmer is to swim freestyle (using the front crawl) continuously for 1/2 mile. This may take you 30 minutes or so at the beginning, and for many people swimming continuously for 30 minutes is quite an effort. The key is to swim at a constant pace, paying attention to your heart rate or your perceived exertion, so that you can continue the effort for the full distance. Take long, relaxed strokes, try-

ing to get as much distance per stroke as possible.

As you go up and down the lengths of the pool, you may want to concentrate on one element of your stroke at a time. So, for the first few lengths, you might concentrate on taking long strokes. Then, for the next few lengths, concentrate on proper breathing technique. Next, concentrate on small, efficient kicks with your legs. Thinking about one element at a time will improve your overall stroke efficiency.

If building up to the 1/2 mile goal proves too difficult, you can split up your lap swimming by doing some of your laps with a kickboard or pull-buoy, and by taking brief rests at the end of several laps. Rests should be just long enough to bring your heart rate down to a comfortable level.

A beginner's workout including the kickboard might look like this:

BEGINNER WORKOUT 1

Warm-up	100 yards, easy and relaxed pace, concentrating on long strokes and an easy pace
Drill	100 yards any stroke
Main	300 yards freestyle, concentrating on efficient stroke and breathing technique
Kick	100 yards with kickboard
Sprint	50 yards / 10 second pause Repeat the 50 yard sprint
Cool-down	100 yards easy freestyle

The total distance of this workout is 800 yards, which is approximately 1/2 mile. The workout can be broken up if 800 yards is too far to go. You could drop the 300-yard freestyle swim to only 200 yards, or you could take out the drill or kickboard set.

Here is a somewhat more varied and challenging 800-yard workout:

BEGINNER WORKOUT 2

Warm-up	100 yards freestyle
Drill	50 yards any stroke
Main	200 yards moderate freestyle
	50 yards backstroke
	100 yards faster freestyle
	50 yards backstroke
	50 yards maximum-effort freestyle
Kick	100 yards fast with kickboard
Cool-down	100 yards easy freestyle

Total distance: 800 yards

Insert brief rests wherever you need them.

Intermediate Workout

Once you can comfortably swim 1/2 mile without taking rest periods, you should work up to one mile (approximately 1800 yards). You want to raise your workout distances gradually, so you might aim for a 1200-yard total workout for one week or two, then a 1600-yard total workout for another week or two, and then finally move to your 1800-yard goal. Sample intermediate workouts might look like the following (all strokes are freestyle unless otherwise noted):

INTERMEDIATE WORKOUT 1

Warm-up	200 yards freestyle
Drill	100 yards any stroke
Main	200 yards with negative split (the second 100 yards is swum faster than the first) /10 sec. pause
	50 yards any stroke / 5 sec. pause
	Repeat Main set again
Kick	200 yards with kickboard, alternating laps of slow and fast pace
Sprint	100 yards any stroke, maximum intensity
Cool-down	100 yards easy freestyle

Total distance: 1200 yards

Here's a bit more challenging intermediate-level workout:

INTERMEDIATE WORKOUT 2

Warm-up	200 yards freestyle
Drill	100 yards any stroke
Main	300 yards, moderate pace
	50 yards easy / 50 yards fast
	200 yards, any stroke moderate pace
	50 yards, easy / 50 yards, fast
Kick	200 yards, any stroke
Pull	200 yards, negative split
Sprint	50 yards, maximum intensity pause 10 seconds repeat
Cool-down	100 yards easy freestyle

Total distance: 1600 yards

When you are ready, you want to swim 1800 yards free-style without stopping. Once you can swim this one-mile distance continuously, your endurance will be strong enough so that you can move on to sprint training or long-distance swimming.

Advanced Workout— Building Speed

All aerobic training is based upon the theory that if we overload our cardiovascular systems, they will grow stronger to meet the demand. As such, our goal in swimming is not just to be able to swim one mile or longer at any slow pace, but rather to stress our cardiovascular systems so that they learn to work harder and we are able to swim faster. One of the best ways to do this is to incorporate interval training so that our heart rates are elevated higher than they would be in regular endurance swimming.

Interval training in swimming involves alternating periods of higher-effort swimming with brief periods of rest or periods of controlled, slower swimming. These lower-effort periods allow you to recover from the near all-out swimming without letting your heart rate drop completely. Interval training will benefit you whether you are trying to swim longer or faster.

One method for setting your intervals is to tell yourself that you will swim as fast as you can for a given length of time, and then allow yourself a set period of time for rest or lower-effort swimming (say 5 or 10 seconds). An interval can also consist of a distance goal instead of a time goal, such as swimming two near-maximum lengths of the pool and then one restful length.

The rest interval will vary according to your training goals and needs. Shorter rest periods are usually for the swimmer who wants to build more endurance. Longer rest periods are for the swimmer who wants to work on speed, who will go all-out or nearly all-out in the speed part of the interval.

The following is a sample interval workout for the swimmer who wants to increase his speed (all strokes are freestyle unless otherwise noted):

ADVANCED WORKOUT

Warm-up	300 yards freestyle
Drill	100 yards any stroke
Main	50 yards, easy pace / 5 sec. rest
	50 yards faster pace / 5 sec. rest
	50 yards near-maximum pace / 5 sec. rest
	100 yards moderate pace
	Repeat 4 times
Kick	200 yards, any stroke
Pull	200 yards, moderate pace / 10 sec. rest
Sprint	100 yards, fast pace
	50 yards, maximum effort
	10 seconds rest
	50 yards, maximum effort
Cool-down	100 yards easy freestyle

Total distance: 2100 yards

Non-Swimming Water Aerobics

There are plenty of other ways to work out in water besides swimming. In fact, if you stay in shallow water, you don't even have to know how to swim to do them.

Physical therapists have been instructing disabled people and injured people in water exercises for nearly a century, and water aerobics' popularity has grown immensely in the 80s and 90s. In fact, almost every pool open to the public, especially those at health clubs, now offers some form of water aerobics classes. They have names like Aquaerobics, Aquacize, Waterobics, and so on. The classes are usually smaller than traditional aerobics classes, and the teacher is either in the water with the students or on the edge of the pool deck demonstrating the exercises. Music is often incorporated with the movements, and students will use various training devices and weights as well as their own bodies' weight in water to create resistance.

The resistance of water is twelve to fourteen times greater than air, so even just walking along the bottom of a chest-high swimming pool is twelve to fourteen times more exercise than walking on dry ground. But you feel far less impact on your body, because about ninety percent of your weight is buoyant. This means that the work is hard, but the strain on joints is minimal. Serious land runners often use in-water running as a means of training and rehabilitating after an injury. Many runners have found that their times actually improve after substituting water running for land running.

Here is a water aerobics routine you can follow without going to an organized class. I have divided the routine into two parts: an aerobics portion and conditioning exercises. Before getting into the water, follow the Warm-Up Routine on page 61.

AEROBICS AND LOWER BODY CONDITIONING

Water running

▶Run in place in the pool in chest- or waist-deep water, being sure to swing your arms as if you were running on land. Raise your knees high—like an exaggerated march.

20x each leg slow/20x each leg medium/20x each leg fast

Jumping jacks

▶ 20x slow/20x medium/20x fast

Strides

▶Take long strides, using your arms to propel you off the pool floor.

20x slow/20x medium/20x fast

Jump Up

►Jump bringing both knees to your chest, pushing your arms down through the water to your sides.

20x slow/20x medium/20x fast

Straight leg kicks to the front

▶Lean your body slightly backwards and kick each leg to the front.

20x each leg slow/20x each leg medium/20x each leg fast

Leg kicks to the back

▶Lean your body slightly forward and kick each leg to the back.

20x each leg slow/20x each leg medium /20x each leg fast

▶Go back to Water Running (page 208) and repeat the entire sequence three times.

WATER CONDITIONING AND UPPER BODY

Front Press

▶ *Chest and shoulders*

With open palms, bent elbows and arms resting on top of the water, squeeze your elbows and hands toward each other in the water. Then bring them back to the starting position on top of the water.

Perform two sets of 20 repetitions each.

Tricep Extensions

▶ *Triceps*

Stand with your elbows bent, palms facing downward, arms close to your sides. Push your hands through the water and behind you, straightening out your elbows.

Perform one set of 20 repetitions.

Bicep curl

▶ *Biceps*

Stand with your arms straight, palms facing away from you. Push hard with your open palms, moving them up toward your shoulders through the water.

Perform one set of 20 repetitions.

Back Press

▶ *Back*

Stand with your arms out in front of you, palms facing down into the water. Push water to the back from the center line of your body, squeezing your shoulder blades together.

Perform one set of 20 repetitions.

Oblique twist

▶ *Waist*

Twist your torso from side to side in the water, alternating one arm pushing out in front of you and one elbow in by your waist.

Perform one set of 20 repetitions for each side of the body.

About the Authors

Gilad Janklowicz' philosophy and techniques for fitness and health have inspired thousands of people around the world. Gilad was the Israeli national decathlon champion in 1973 and came to the United States in 1980 to train for the Olympics, when an Achilles heel injury ended his competitive career. He turned to aerobic exercise to keep in shape and soon was working in Los Angeles as a fitness trainer to the stars. In 1981 he moved to Honolulu, and by 1985 his televised exercise show *Bodies in Motion* was being shown around the world. *Bodies in Motion* is the top rated fitness show on ESPN, with a viewership of more than 70 million people in 50 different countries.

Ann Marie Brown is a writer, editor and aerobics instructor who lives in San Francisco, California. She is an American Council on Exercise certified fitness instructor who has taught aerobics and weight training classes for more than ten years in Los Angeles and San Francisco.

Get Your BODIES IN MOTION! *with* GILAD

CALL 1-800-322-0664

he host and producer of *Bodies in Motion,* America's #1 fitness program on ESPN, bring his workouts to you
home video! Each tape provides a safe exercise workout for beginner to advanced levels.

Bodies in Motion II
Gilad's 60 & 30 Minute Low Impact Workouts
Two complete low impact aerobic workouts that include a warm-up, low impact aerobic
workout, strength and toning segment and a cool-down. The 30-minute workout is for
the beginner and the 60-minute workout is for the more advanced.

Bodies in Motion IV
Gilad's 45/45 Split Routine Workout
Two complete workouts for intermediate to advanced levels. The Fat Burning
Workout starts with a warm-up, then 30 minutes of low and high impact
aerobics and finishes with a cool-down. The Toning Workout contains a warm-
up, 30 minutes of toning all major muscle groups and a good stretch segment.

Bodies in Motion V
Gilad's Interval Training for Men
A 60-minute workout taped on Oahu's North Shore and designed specifically for
men's strengths and natural abilities. It contains a warm-up, cardiovascular
intervals, strength training circuits and a cool-down and stretch.

Bodies in Motion VI
Gilad's Step Aerobics
A 60-minute workout featuring 35 minutes of fat-burning aerobics using a
Step II bench and a BONUS abdominal segment. The workout starts with a
full body warm-up and finishes with a relaxing cool-down.

Basic Training with Ada
A 60-minute low impact aerobic and strength training workout set on an
action-packed airstrip in Hawaii. The workout includes a warm-up, low impact aerobics,
strength training and toning and a total body stretch. Light weights are recommended.

ES, I would like to order the following tapes:

odies in Motion Vol. II (VHS)   Qty___
odies in Motion Vol. IV (VHS)   Qty___
odies in Motion Vol. V (VHS)   Qty___
odies in Motion Vol. VI (VHS)   Qty___
asic Training with Ada (VHS)   Qty___

y one tape is $49.95, any two for $79.95, any
ee for $99.95, any four for $119.95, or all five
$139.95.
ease add $4 shipping and handling to any size
der. PA residents must add 6% sales tax. HI
sidents must add 4.167% sales tax.

TO ORDER, CALL 1-800-322-0664 *or:*
Send check or money order payable to *Bodies in Motion*
or charge to your Visa/MasterCard/American Express:
Credit Card #_____Exp.____
Signature_____
Name_____
Address_____
_____
Telephone_____

Mail to: *Bodies in Motion,* 1000 Napor Boulevard,
       Pittsburgh, PA 15205